The Good Humor Man

Man

Tales of Life, Laughter and, for Dessert, Ice Cream

Jerry Zezima

DEDICATION

To my humor heroes, the three B's: Robert Benchley, Art Buchwald, and Erma Bombeck.

ACKNOWLEDGMENTS

To my family, which has put up with my stupid jokes for lo these many years and whose various members — principally my wife, Sue — have elevated eye-rolling to an art form.

And to Katie Foran-McHale, Zach Finken, Aaron Gilman, and Christina St. Joseph of Tribune News Service for lowering their otherwise high standards by distributing my humor column to six hundred newspapers nationwide and abroad. Now you know why the entire industry is in trouble.

ALSO BY JERRY ZEZIMA

"Leave It to Boomer: A Look at Life, Love and Parenthood by the Very Model of the Modern Middle-Age Man"

"The Empty Nest Chronicles: How to Have Fun (and Stop Annoying Your Spouse) After the Kids Move Out"

"Grandfather Knows Best: A Geezer's Guide to Life, Immaturity, and Learning How to Change Diapers All Over Again"

"Nini and Poppie's Excellent Adventures: Grandkids, Wine Clubs, and Other Ways to Keep Having Fun"

"Every Day Is Saturday: Sleeping Late, Playing With the Grandchildren, Surviving the Quarantine, and Other Joys of Retirement"

"One for the Ageless: How to Stay Young and Immature Even If You're Really Old"

PRAISE FOR JERRY ZEZIMA

"Zezima is a natural storyteller, never more delightful than when readers suspect he might be, shall we say, exaggerating. His comic timing is impeccable, and it's neatly balanced with his self-deprecating humor."

— Kirkus Reviews

"Fans of humorous essays about real life will be thoroughly entertained by Zezima's quips and insights."

— BookLife Reviews

"I was a fan of Jerry Zezima's hilarious columns in my local newspaper long before I met him. His commentary on daily life, parenting, and now grandparenting has always made me laugh."

— Amy Newmark, publisher, "Chicken Soup for the Soul"

"That Jerry Zezima is one funny guy! Or maybe two. Who knows? I've never actually seen him in person."

— Brian Crane, Reuben Award-winning cartoonist and creator of the syndicated comic strip "Pickles"

"Who could envision Jerry Zezima emerging as the Will Rogers of retirement? Only anyone who's ever read his laugh-out-loud columns on the absurdities of daily life."

— Kevin Cowherd, New York Times bestselling author of "Hothead"

"Jerry Zezima's columns are terrific."

"The theory of 'nominative determinism' posits that one's name charts one's professional destiny. Chuck Yeager, steely test pilot. Florence Nightingale, founder of modern nursing. Mick Jagger, swaggering rock and roll frontman. When charting his direction in the world, Jerry Zezima had absolutely no choice in his life's role as written-word humorist. In person, Jerry's warm, self-deprecating wit is infectious. Everything he says is carefully crafted to make you laugh, and his columns (which I've been reading since I was a high schooler in Connecticut) are natural extensions of his gleefully playful personality. I honestly can't really give him any credit for his decades of making people smile, though. As the moniker suggests, Jerry Zezima just can't help it."

"Jerry Zezima is the king of family humor, Erma Bombeck's male counterpart."

Contents

DEDICATION..iii

ACKNOWLEDGMENTS...iv

ALSO BY JERRY ZEZIMA v

PRAISE FOR JERRY ZEZIMA vi

INTRODUCTION...xiii

CHAPTER 1: "CHILD'S PLAY".. 1

"The Cold Facts About Ice Cream" 1

"Diary of a Silly Grandfather" 3

"The Playground Grandpa" 7

"The Rise and Fall of a Real Klutz".............................. 10

"The Carousel Stakes"... 12

"The Fab Five" 14

CHAPTER 2: "HOME, SWEAT HOME"............................ 17

"Paint Misbehavin' " 17

"Jerry, Jerry, Quite Contrary" 19

"The Dish on Dishwashers" 21

"Food for Naught".. 24

"Cause for Alarm" 26

"An Open and Shut Case" 29

"I Married a Cover Girl" 32

"Here's Looking at You, Pal" 34

"Coming Clean About Vacuums" 36

"Little Kitchen of Horrors" 38

CHAPTER 3: "MORE KID STUFF" 42

"Rub-a-Dub-Dub, One Kid in the Tub" 42

"Math Confusion" 44

"In the Jurassic Dark" 47

"A Grand Decade" 49

"Nothing but the Tooth" 52

"Home Is Where the Art Is" 54

"Not Exactly the Bee's Knees" 56

"Funeral for a Fish" 59

"The Early Bird Gets the Lemonade" 61

"Rave Restaurant Review" 63

CHAPTER 4: "IT'S A GUY THING" 66

"If the Pants Fit, Wear Them" 66

"The Grandpa Grilling Club" 68

"Bye Bye Birdie Droppings" 71

"You've Still Got Mail" 74

"Eat, Drink and Be Married" 76

"Bathroom Remodeling Is a Real Soap Opera" 79

"Air to a Fortune" 81

"House of the Rising Cost" 83

"Martha and Me" 85

"Bristle Boy Blue" 88

"The Taming of the Screw" 90

"I Shopped and Didn't Drop" 92

CHAPTER 5: "OUTSIDE CHANCES" 96

"The Strawberry Whisperer" 96

"The Empty Nesters" 98

"The Great Egg Mystery" 101

"A Sod Story" 104

"The Garden of Eatin' " 107

CHAPTER 6: "DIAL 'M' FOR MADNESS" 109

"Warranty Calls Are an Auto Motive" 109

"Hack to the Future".. 111

"Headed Off at the Password"..................................... 114

"The Buzz on Beeps" 116

CHAPTER 7: "WHAT'S UP, DOCS?".......................... 119

"The Big Stuff Theory"... 119

"Our Potholes Are Out of This World"..................... 121

"These Folks Are Good Medicine" 125

"The Sound of Joking" 130

"Just What the Doctors Ordered" 132

"Going Viral" 135

"Off-the-Cuff Remarks"... 137

CHAPTER 8: "MISCELLANEOUS MUSINGS" 141

"Hooked on Crocheting"... 141

"I Need Moe Money" 144

"Raised Seal of Approval" 146

"You Axed for It".. 149

"Those Are the Brakes"... 152

"Getting Trivial With Alexa" 155

"Some People Have All the Luck"............................... 158

"That's the Ticket".. 160

"A Second Helping of a Winning Recipe"............................. 163

CHAPTER 9: "THE ICING ON THE CAKE"........................ 167

"All Aboard the Polar Express" 167

"Flaky the Snowman" 169

"How Sweet It Was" 172

"Ice Cream Guy Keeps on Truckin' " 177

EPILOGUE 181

INTRODUCTION

You scream, I scream, we all scream for …

Beer!

Well, I do when the kiddies aren't around.

But when it comes to sweet treats, my five grandchildren love nothing more than ice cream. Their favorite is a towering cone of vanilla or chocolate soft serve — topped with rainbow sprinkles — which invariably melts in the summer sun and drips onto their clothes or gets smeared all over their faces, requiring me to mop up the mess with a dozen of those wimpy little napkins that I then stuff into an overflowing trash bin with big grandpa hands sticky with the remnants of an afternoon's pleasure.

Ice cream may not be the answer to all our problems, but it is a delightful diversion in both the best of times and the worst of times. And lately, for many people, it has indeed been the worst of times. Read the paper or watch the news and you will think the world is going to hell in a handbasket. (Note to self: Get into the handbasket business. And make the product fireproof.)

That's why we could use a heaping helping of both Good Humor (one of my favorite ice cream brands) and good humor (which I write in a nationally syndicated newspaper column).

Like ice cream, this book won't solve all your problems, but it will give you a welcome respite from all the bad stuff going on these days.

I write about everything from trying to buy paint from a color-blind salesman to bouncing on a trampoline with the grandkids, from picking fruit with the Strawberry Whisperer to building the world's most pathetic snowman, from participating in a Three Stooges auction to helping out in the garden and getting hit in the head by my own rake.

I even write about — you guessed it — ice cream.

This book is filled with true stories of family foibles and the funny little things of everyday life.

The star of the proceedings is my wife, Sue. She's the backbone of the family and the brains of the outfit. She's also a sweet, beautiful, eternally patient woman who, for putting up with me for more than four decades, deserves to be the first living person canonized by the Catholic Church. I deserve to be shot from a cannon.

Then there are our daughters, Katie and Lauren, and their husbands, Dave and Guillaume, successful and well-adjusted people who love me even though they react to my stupid jokes by rolling their eyes like pinwheels and who have resigned themselves to the immutable fact that my main mission in life is to corrupt their children.

That brings me to those very same kids, the ones who love ice cream so much, our smart, funny, adorable, talented, fantastic, wonderful (you get the idea) grandchildren: Chloe and Lilly, who are Lauren and Guillaume's daughters, and Xavier, Zoe, and Quinn, who are Katie and Dave's children. I am, if I may be permitted to brag, their favorite toy.

You might even see yourself in here. Whether you are a spouse, a parent, a grandparent, or all of the above, you have no doubt gone through the same kind of stuff I have. I just take things one step further than any normal person would take them because, of course, I'm not normal.

But you don't have to be a nationally syndicated newspaper columnist to know that the ability to find the humor in life can be the sweetest treat of all.

So sit back with this book, open a carton of ice cream, grab a spoon, and dig in.

And make sure you have plenty of napkins.

CHAPTER 1:
"CHILD'S PLAY"

"The Cold Facts About Ice Cream"

As a journalist, I have always enjoyed getting a scoop. As an ice cream fan, I got a scoop that turned out to have a chilling effect: It's hard to eat this sweet treat when the air temperature is colder than your ice cream.

That's the lesson I learned when I took Chloe and Lilly for their first ice cream outing of the season.

Also on this arctic expedition were Sue and Lauren.

According to the weather app on my phone, it was forty-two degrees. But with the windchill, the nefarious meteorological gauge designed to make hapless ice cream lovers even colder, the "real-feel" temp was at the freezing mark: thirty-two.

This did not deter Chloe, who gazed up at me with wide eyes and pleaded, "Poppie, let's go for ice cream!"

To which Lilly added, through chattering teeth, "Come on!"

Then, in unison, they sang, "You scream, I scream, we all scream for ice cream!"

I felt like screaming when my nose hairs started to stiffen in the brisk breeze.

But I didn't want to disappoint the girls, who the previous week had missed the ice cream truck's first appearance of the year.

We were in their house when the chirpy yet annoyingly monotonous jingle rang outside.

"Poppie, the ice cream truck!" Chloe shrieked.

"Let's go!" Lilly chimed in.

I ran outside in my stocking feet (I wasn't actually wearing stockings, which are a lot more stylish than the smelly socks I had on) only to see the ice cream truck rounding the corner.

"No!" cried Lilly.

"Run after it, Poppie!" urged Chloe.

I didn't want the girls to think their big, strong grandfather has tender tootsies, which is really the case, but I convinced them that I had a better chance of running down the truck — without, I fervently hoped, being run down myself — if I went back inside and put on my sneakers.

I emerged shod in shoddy shoes, which didn't do any good because the truck didn't seem to be returning. Still, I heard its faint song playing on the next street.

"Call for the ice cream man to come back, Poppie!" Chloe begged.

"Yell!" Lilly yelled.

I took a deep breath and, with all my hot air, shouted, "Ice cream man, come baaaaack!"

He didn't hear me. A moment later, I saw the truck roll down an intersecting street on its way to another neighborhood.

The girls were crestfallen. I was, too, since I had a sudden hankering for a vanilla soft serve.

That's why, when I had the chance to redeem myself and play ice cream hero, I said what I always say when the girls ask me for something: "Of course!"

You can't say I'm not a strict grandpa.

So the girls and I, along with Sue and Lauren, went to a nearby ice cream parlor where Chloe and Lilly are regular summertime customers.

The only problem was that it isn't summer. It's spring. And

it felt like winter. Or at least fall.

We had the four seasons. I'm surprised Frankie Valli wasn't along for the ride.

Lauren and the girls got out of their car; Sue and I got out of ours. We went to the window and ordered a vanilla soft serve cone with rainbow sprinkles for Chloe, a cup of chocolate ice cream with chocolate sprinkles for Lilly, and a cup of vanilla soft serve without sprinkles (because I was driving) for yours truly.

Sue, who has ice cream for dessert every night after dinner (she puts it in the microwave for five seconds), was too cold to order a cup. So was Lauren.

I was a tad chilly myself, even though I wore a fleece that wouldn't have prevented a polar bear from freezing to death.

So we all piled into Lauren's car, which had the heat on, and spooned, licked, and slurped our sweet treats in the first outing of the season.

Here's another scoop: Ice cream is always better when it's warm enough to sit outside and eat it.

"Diary of a Silly Grandfather"

If I have learned one thing as a father and a grandfather, aside from the important fact that maturity is best left to young people, it's that kids grow up fast. This is what happens when you feed them.

And if you think your kids grow up fast, wait until you have grandchildren.

That's what Sue and I discovered when we visited Katie, Dave, Xavier, Zoe, and Quinn.

Because of the pandemic, we hadn't seen them in ten months. And before that, we hadn't seen them in a year and a half. Considering Xavier is about to turn five and Zoe and her twin brother, Quinn, will soon be three, Sue and I have missed a lot.

But we made up for lost time on this visit, a diary of which appears below.

Thursday

Sue and I drive almost three hundred miles for our much-anticipated get-together. We marvel at how much the twins have grown. They speak in complete sentences and actually make sense, which distinguishes them from yours truly.

Xavier beams when he sees us and exclaims, "Hi, Nini! Hi, Poppie!"

He's tall, sweet, and handsome. We hug and kiss him.

Then I take all three kids downstairs to play. After dinner, everyone has ice cream. When the children go to bed, the adults have wine.

It's going to be a great week.

Friday

Sue, Katie, and I walk Xavier to school. Then we walk back, get in Katie's car, and make an exciting trip to the supermarket.

Back at the house, I play hide-and-seek with Zoe and Quinn, who tell me where to hide so they can find me.

"You have to hide in a very specific spot," Dave informs me.

Before the kids go to bed, I sit with all of them and watch Xavier's favorite show, "PAW Patrol," an animated series about hero dogs. Over the course of a week, I see about eighty-seven episodes. I still can't get the theme song out of my otherwise empty skull.

Saturday

We go to the zoo. Zoe brings a toy vacuum cleaner, which she uses in front of the great ape exhibit.

"She'll have a lot to clean up when she gets inside," the

father of a baby says as we stand in line.

"Just wait until she sees the elephants," I respond.

Unfortunately, the tusked titans are nowhere to be found because it's too cold for them to be outside.

"They must have packed their trunks and gone to Florida," I remark.

But we do see a bunch of creepy crawlers in the reptile house, where Quinn waves to a snake.

"I don't think he can wave back," I tell him.

Undeterred, Quinn says, "Hi, snake!"

He calls the turtles, crocodiles, and lizards "cute."

Back outside, Quinn is delighted by the ducks, cows, alpacas, and otters, but he's not too enamored of the seals and sea lions, which he says are "scary."

As we are leaving, Zoe shouts, "See you later, alligator!"

When we get back, Xavier helps Sue bake cupcakes. It's a sweet end to a busy day.

Sunday

After breakfast, I take the twins downstairs and start playing with a soccer ball.

"That's for outside," Zoe says firmly. "This one," she adds, handing me a smaller ball, "is for inside."

"Despite evidence to the contrary," Dave says, "they do listen."

We spend the day outside, where we have — that's right — a ball.

When we get back, Dave beats me in Strat-O-Matic, a baseball board game. It's a sad reminder of why I never made it past Little League.

Monday

Zoe is up at five a.m. Bright-tailed and bushy-eyed, so am I.

We color with crayons for a while. Xavier gets up at six-thirty.

At seven o'clock, Quinn is still sleeping.

"WE HAVE TO BE QUIET!" Zoe shouts.

Two minutes later, Quinn is wide awake.

I change the twins' diapers — I'm a hands-on grandfather — before everyone gets dressed so we can go out. Zoe and Quinn are in the seats of their double stroller and Xavier is on the running board. I push the stroller — super fast! — with all three children aboard. When we get back, I take a nap.

Later, we all go to a family-friendly brewery that has toys for the kids and beverages for the adults.

"Cheers!" I say, clinking glasses with Katie, Dave, and Sue. "It's too bad they don't serve beer in sippy cups."

Tuesday

Katie, Sue, and I take Xavier to a nice pizzeria for lunch. Then we go to the Children's Museum.

"Are children on display?" I wonder.

"No," Sue replies. "But you should be."

It's a fantastic place with interactive exhibits. Xavier has a great time, especially with the trains.

"What did you like best, buddy?" Katie asks him as we are leaving.

"All of it!" is his enthusiastic reply.

At bedtime, Katie gathers all three children and reads a hilarious book called "Dog Breath."

Xavier turns to me and says, "Don't forget to brush your

teeth, Poppie."

Wednesday

It's the last day of our visit, which has gone by way too fast. As Xavier gets ready to go to day camp, he says to Sue, "You and Poppie won't be here when I get back, will you?"

It brings a tear to the eye. We hug and kiss him. We do the same with Zoe and Quinn.

But we've had a memorable visit. Sue, who is recovering from a heart attack, couldn't pick up the kids or push them in the stroller, but she has enjoyed every minute. So have I.

We thank Katie and Dave and head out to the car.

Seeing them all again after such a long time has done Sue's heart — and mine — a world of good.

"The Playground Grandpa"

Because I am a relic from another time (the time right now is 10:47 a.m.), I am known to my grandchildren as a dinosaur. I am also known — at least at a park where I brought Zoe and Quinn for some fun and frolic — as the Playground Grandpa.

This appropriate appellation was bestowed upon me by a guy who had broken his foot and couldn't run around with his six-year-old son. That job fell to me after the kid, the twins, and a bunch of other youngsters wanted me to chase them in the broiling sun, watch them go down the slide, and otherwise act as silly as I do even when I'm not around munchkins six decades my junior.

"You're the Playground Grandpa," the fracture-footed father said as I stopped to catch my breath, which at that point must have smelled something awful.

This sentiment was echoed by the mother of three young boys who joined my crazy antics. They especially liked it when I engaged them in a game of sticks, wherein I held a small stick in my right hand, looked at the kids gathered to the left of me, and said no one was going to take it away. Meanwhile, one of the brothers would sneak around to the other side and snatch the stick from my fingers. My shameless double takes and looks of wide-eyed surprise sent the elated assemblage into gales of laughter each of the approximately two dozen times I repeated the nonsense.

"Thank you very much," the mom said when it was time to go home. "They had fun with you."

"You're very welcome," I responded. "That's because I'm less mature than any of them."

Zoe and Quinn, who are about to turn three, weren't jealous at all.

"Follow me," I sang as we went back to the car. "I'm the Pied Poppie."

I'm also the prehistoric Poppie because the dynamic duo and their big brother, Xavier, who's five, are into dinosaurs — especially, of course, me.

"Am I a dinosaur?" I asked them.

Zoe: "Yes!"

Quinn: "Yes!"

Xavier: "Maybe."

All three know their prehistoric creatures, pictures of which adorn their backpacks, lunch boxes, and clothing. They also watch TV shows — "Steve and Maggie" and "Blippi" are the most popular — with dinosaur themes. After hearing that the kids like T. rex the best, I said my favorite is the woolly mammoth.

Xavier sighed and said, "That's a different era, Poppie."

I went in one era and out the other when Xavier and I spent an afternoon at what he calls the Dinosaur Museum, where we saw fossils (something I do when I look in the bathroom mirror to shave) and lots of other neat stuff, including an exhibit on early humans. I must say that the likeness between one of the cave dwellers and a certain modern grandfather was remarkable.

Even more remarkable was my repeat performance as the Playground Grandpa when Dave and I took Zoe and Quinn to another park the next day.

As soon as we arrived, a seven-year-old boy came up to me and said, "Wanna see how fast I can run?"

"Sure," I told him.

"I bet you can't run as fast as I can," he said.

"I bet I can," I replied.

The slender speedster immediately took off with me in hot (because I was sweating profusely) pursuit.

When her son finally stopped, and with me on the verge of collapse, his mother smiled and said, "You have a way with kids."

"They have a way with me," I gasped, the words coming in short bursts as I imagined first responders giving me PGR (Playground Grandpa Resuscitation).

A second seven-year-old came up to me and started a rambling conversation in which he informed me that he had superpowers and came from a family of wolves.

Then he started kicking a soccer ball around with me and finished by actually laughing at my atrocious puns, which his mother, who played soccer in high school, called "dad jokes."

"My dad tells them, too," the kid said.

"Do you think mine are funny?" I asked.

"Yes!" he gushed.

"Good," I said. "Tell your dad you heard them from the Playground Grandpa."

"The Rise and Fall of a Real Klutz"

Being a grandfather has put a bounce in my step, frequently followed by a stubbed toe, but I really got a jump on fun when my granddaughters invited me to join them on their new trampoline.

I've had my ups and downs over the years, but I had never been on a trampoline, even when I was the girls' age. That's why Chloe, a third-grader, and Lilly, a kindergartner, were happy to help me reach new heights of giddiness when the three of us cavorted on the springy circular device that was recently erected in their backyard.

"You'll have a blast, Poppie!" Chloe promised.

"Don't fall on your face!" Lilly added thoughtfully.

Sue and I hadn't seen the girls in a couple of months, so we drove to their house for Family Movie Night, which included pizza for dinner, ice pops for dessert, and homemade popcorn to munch on while watching "School of Rock," which was selected by Lauren.

"I love rock and roll!" Chloe exclaimed while dancing in front of the TV.

"Rock on, dude!" Lilly chimed in.

Right after Sue and I arrived, we watched parts of "Encanto," which Lilly said she had seen "one hundred and sixty-nine times."

She and Chloe got up and boogied to the popular animated movie.

Then we cackled while watching cartoons starring Wile E. Coyote and the Road Runner.

"The Acme Company has a lot of crazy products," Chloe observed after the Coyote had received several orders from that esteemed corporation.

"The poor Coyote," Lilly said sympathetically when one of those products blew up in the luckless canine's face.

It all set the stage, before we sent out for pizza, for fun on the trampoline.

"Take off your shoes, Poppie," Chloe instructed from inside the trampoline, which was surrounded by netting to prevent a clumsy person ("like you, Poppie," Lilly emphasized) from bouncing off the synthetic sheet, doing a somersault that would have earned a perfect score in a gymnastics competition, and banging his head on the hard ground, in which case the aforementioned klutz would be even dizzier than usual.

"Just like the Coyote when he falls off a cliff," Chloe reminded me.

I doffed my sneakers and slowly climbed onto the trampoline, where I immediately developed rubber legs. I felt like a Weeble, except that, according to the commercial song for the famous roly-poly toys, "Weebles wobble, but they don't fall down."

I fell down.

When I got up, I started to bounce with the girls. It was exhilarating — until I fell down again.

"Let's play Ring Around the Rosie!" Chloe said.

"How about Ring Around the Poppie?" Lilly suggested.

We sang the lyrics with my name and, at the end, we all fell down.

The merriment continued as we danced to more songs and circumnavigated the trampoline while each of us hopped on one foot. We also skipped, slipped, and tripped.

In every case, I ended up on my keister.

"Attack Poppie!" the girls cried in unison before jumping as high as they could and landing with full force on my fallen form.

It took my breath away.

Half an hour later, we called it quits. I wasn't good enough as a trampoliner to be in the Olympics, or even to join the circus, although I might have made it as a clown. But I did, as Chloe predicted, have a blast.

"You're more fun than the Road Runner and the Coyote," she told me.

"And," Lilly added, "you didn't fall off a cliff."

"The Carousel Stakes"

I'm way too old to be a jockey, but I like to horse around, which makes me a champion with my granddaughters. And I proved it on a carousel in a photo finish with Chloe and Lilly, who accompanied me to the winner's circle in our very own version of the Kentucky Derby.

I may never make it to Churchill Downs, at least not as a rider, but I was once involved in a fateful race at Belmont Park.

Shortly after Sue and I were married, we went to the New York racetrack, where two memorable things happened: Sue got sunstroke and I bet on a horse that dropped dead.

In one of the races, I placed a two-dollar bet on a horse named Life's Hope. Sue bet the same amount on a horse with no name. (Actually, he did have a name, but I forget what it was.)

The equine sprinters broke from the starting gate with Sue's horse in the lead. He led from start to finish.

"I won!" squealed Sue, whose payoff was a whopping five bucks.

"Hey," I said, "what happened to Life's Hope? I didn't see him cross the finish line."

Just then, an ambulance raced across the track. My suspicions were confirmed: My horse never made it out of the starting gate. Life's Hope had neither life nor hope.

Sue ended up in slightly better shape with sunstroke.

After that, we stopped going to the track.

But years later, I took a riding lesson at a stable where I proved to be unstable in the saddle of a gelding named Bob, who was appropriately named because he bobbed along as I held the reins tightly and worried that he was still smarting from his surgery.

"You have to learn how to steer him," said Julie, the instructor, who assured me that Bob had fully recovered from his operation and was perfectly comfortable giving me a ride.

"He's the mane man," I remarked. "And if he stopped short, I'd be saved by the driver's-side hair bag."

That didn't happen because Bob was very gentle. In fact, we had a male (of sorts) bonding.

The lesson proved valuable when I rode in the Carousel Stakes with Chloe and Lilly.

It was a crowded field, with about two dozen jockeys on the backs of the wooden Thoroughbreds. Among the spectators was Sue, who didn't wager two dollars on a horse but did give the attendant five bucks — her winnings at Belmont — for tickets.

The girls and I each climbed onto a horse. Chloe, riding a filly she dubbed Checkers, got up by herself. Lilly needed a boost from me to get onto Sparkle. I struggled to get mounted on Mustard.

Most of the riders were, like the girls, of elementary school age. Others were young parents. I was clearly the oldest. From the looks I got, I'm surprised I wasn't put out to pasture.

"This will be fun, Poppie!" Chloe told me.

"Hold on tight!" Lilly chimed in.

"My horse is going to win," I predicted.

"No, he's not!" Lilly shot back. "Mine is."

"No, mine is," Chloe said.

All three horses were lined up perfectly with each other. Suddenly, the music started. It wasn't the bugle call of the Kentucky Derby. And no track announcer exclaimed, "They're off!"

But the horses started moving anyway.

"Go, Checkers!" Chloe said, urging her horse on.

"Come on," Sparkle!" cried Lilly.

"What's my horse's name?" I asked.

"Mustard," the girls replied in unison.

"Go, Mustard!" I yelled.

Round and round we went, up and down, heading toward the finish line with the horses neck and neck. The crowd roared. Finally, in the closest race in history, it was over — a three-way tie.

"We all won!" Lilly proclaimed.

I dedicated my victory to Life's Hope. Sue was just happy she didn't get sunstroke.

"The Fab Five"

What happens to an immature geezer whose five grandchildren meet for the very first time and spend the better part of a week splashing at the beach, romping at a family reunion, gawking at sea creatures in the aquarium, riding the carousel, going out to lunch, and otherwise having the time of their lives?

Answer: The grandfather has even more fun than the kids do.

The aforementioned geezer, it should be noted, is yours truly. And I am proud, happy, and slightly delirious to say that the child's play did me a lot of good, even though Sue, the kiddies' grandmother, has long known that I'm the biggest and most playful child of them all.

The Fab Five — three girls and two boys — are cousins,

although the oldest two (Chloe and Lilly, who are nine and five years old, respectively) are sisters, and the youngest three (Xavier, five, and twins Zoe and Quinn, three) are siblings.

I may be terrible at math, but I somehow have it figured out.

The adventure began with a visit by Xavier, Zoe, and Quinn, who arrived (with Katie and Dave) after midnight and awoke bright-eyed and bushy-tailed at six a.m., which is more than the grown-ups could say, at least not without large doses of caffeine.

The much-anticipated moment occurred after lunch when we all drove to the home of Chloe and Lilly, who (with Lauren and Guillaume) had met Xavier when he was a toddler but who had never met Zoe and Quinn. They all hit it off immediately, which was wonderful to see, even through heavy-lidded eyes, because the caffeine was starting to wear off.

It was replaced by adrenaline when we went to the beach, where I was the flotation device for kiddies who kicked, bounced, and splashed in the sand, sun, and surf while I attempted to keep my head above water and hoped not to be eaten by a shark.

After a day of drying out (from water, not beer, which was consumed after the kiddies went to bed), we had a family reunion with eighteen people: all five grandchildren; their parents; my mother, Rosina; my sisters, Elizabeth and Susan; Susan's grown children, Taylor, Blair, and Whitney; Taylor's wife, Carlin; and, of course, Sue and yours truly.

It was the first time my mother, who is ninety-seven and is sharper than I am (so are houseplants, but Mom is still impressive), had been together with all of her children, all of her grandchildren, and all of her great-grandchildren. She was the life of the party.

The fun continued the following day when Sue and I went to the aquarium with the five children and their parents. I found out why I wasn't food for sharks at the beach: They were swimming in a huge tank, where they eat fish that are, I am relieved to admit, more appetizing than I am.

Then we went out to lunch at a seafood joint.

"Are sharks on the menu?" I asked the waitress, who looked at me as if the theme from "Jaws" was running through her head: Dumb-dumb, dumb-dumb, dumb-dumb, dumb-dumb.

I had an appetizing fish sandwich instead.

The final full day was spent at the carousel, where the Fab Five rode the horses and tried unsuccessfully to grab the brass ring. On one ride, I leaned over and nearly fell off but managed to get one, which, in the wide eyes of the children, made me — you guessed it — the lord of the rings.

We again went out to lunch before heading back to Chloe and Lilly's house, where the kiddie quintet and I, together and separately, jumped on the trampoline.

My legs were rubbery for the next twenty-four hours, by which time Katie, Dave, Xavier, Zoe, and Quinn had departed for home.

It was a magical week. And the only one to have more fun than the grandkids was a certain immature geezer who proved to be the biggest kid of all.

CHAPTER 2:

"HOME, SWEAT HOME"

"Paint Misbehavin' "

I am off the wall, which is why I like to give the brush-off to stuff that goes on the wall.

By that I mean paint. And, even worse, the process that goes into picking it out.

Color me confused when I go to a paint store, where I end up throwing shade at the thousands of shades of paint that Sue wants me to consider when she is going to pick the one she wants anyway.

That is exactly what happened when Sue said she wanted me to paint both the living room and the dining room, which look good even though I painted them so long ago that the shade of paint I used (a pinkish tone called, I believe, "pinkish tone") has been discontinued.

I knew this was not going to be an easy project when Sue told me that she had already gone to a paint store and had talked with a salesman who said he couldn't help her pick out the right shade of paint because he is — are you ready for this? — color blind.

"You have to go back there with me so I can meet this guy," I told Sue.

When we arrived, we were greeted by a salesman named James.

"Are you color blind?" I asked.

"No," he responded quizzically. "Why?"

"My wife," I said, pointing to Sue, "was in here recently and spoke with a salesman who said he's color blind."

"He was helping this woman who had a million and one questions," Sue explained. "I guess he was overwhelmed. When he got to me, he said the store has eight thousand eight hundred and sixty shades of paint and that he couldn't help me pick out the right one because he's color blind."

"That's insane!" James exclaimed. "He probably made it up because nobody wants to go through all those colors. Unless he's keeping it a secret from me."

"Maybe you can help," Sue said as she looked through several rows of beige and pink samples. "This one," she added, holding up a sample, "is too beige. And this one," she said, pointing to another sample, "is pink teetering on beige."

"What do you think?" James asked me.

"I think I'm bored teetering on senility," I told him.

We all agreed that the problem with paint samples, which aren't much bigger than postage stamps, is that it's almost impossible to tell how a particular color will look on a wall.

That was evident when Sue brought home samples from her first trip to the store and asked me how they looked in the dining room.

"Do you like early sunset?" asked Sue, referring to one of the colors.

"I prefer daylight saving time," I answered.

"You're no help at all," she huffed.

"Thank you," I said.

Back at the store, Sue said she wanted to replicate the color in the dining room and the living room and described it to James.

"It sounds like dogwood," he said.

"That's it!" Sue squeaked.

"I can mix a small can for you to take home," said James,

who added that picking the right color is the toughest part of painting.

"It's very stressful," Sue agreed.

"The painting itself is easy," said James.

"Especially if you have beer," I chimed in.

When the paint was finished being shaken, not stirred, James handed the can to Sue.

"Let me know how it turns out," he said. "If you don't like it, we have thousands of other colors to choose from."

When we got home, Sue found an old paintbrush, opened the can, and brushed some paint on the living room wall.

"It's too light," she said.

"Wait for it to dry," I suggested.

"I'll have to put on a second coat," Sue said.

"Are you cold?" I asked.

Sue shook her head and waited until the next day, when the paint had dried and her head had stopped shaking.

"It's not the right color," Sue announced after she tried again. "But I'm going to find it. We just have to go back to the store and get more samples."

"Don't ask me for any further advice," I said.

"How come?" Sue asked.

"I forgot to tell you," I said. "I'm color blind."

"Jerry, Jerry, Quite Contrary"

When it comes to gardening, I'm a blooming idiot. But that hasn't stopped Sue from enlisting my sorry services in planting vegetables, transplanting plants, and making the flower beds comfy because, as I told her when we went to the landfill for some free topsoil, I work dirt cheap.

As I also told her, there's no tool like an old tool, which explains why, in a pathetic attempt to assist in the beautification of our little piece of earth, I was hit in the head by my own rake.

It happened when I dug a hole with a shovel, another dangerous implement whose main goal in life is to wrench my back, so I could plant a peony that I bought for Sue, not realizing that she would make me stick it in the ground.

This entailed using an iron rake to smooth out the area that would become the peony's home. Or, rather, its temporary home. (More on this in a moment.)

The rake and the shovel must have been in cahoots because, as soon as I dug the hole, I put down the shovel and promptly stepped on the teeth of the rake, which immediately rose up to club me on the cranium.

It's a good thing it didn't smash my teeth, in which case I'd be dealing with roots of another kind. It's also a wonder, considering the thickness of my skull, that the rake didn't break.

Naturally, Sue was very concerned.

"Is the rake OK?" she asked.

It survived the trauma nicely and was ready for more dirty work. But first, Sue and I went to the landfill for the aforementioned topsoil.

"Loam, sweet loam," I cooed.

"Just dig," Sue snapped.

When we got back to the house, I dumped the topsoil into Sue's vegetable garden and smoothed it out with the rake, taking extreme caution against another physical attack.

Usually, our yard runs the botanical gamut from A (azaleas) to Z (zucchini), but this year, Sue isn't planting the latter, which is fine with me because the only thing I would find less appetizing is poison ivy, which I'm not itching to try.

Instead, she planted herbs on the right side of the garden, hot peppers in the middle, and tomatoes on the left, along with string beans and a hyacinth bulb.

"The jalapeño and cayenne peppers will blow your brains out," said Sue, who loves them because she's hot stuff herself.

"They couldn't do that to me," I replied, not even bothering to elaborate. Sue agreed anyway.

Then it was time to plant flowers, notably azaleas and peonies, for which I had to dig holes around the perimeter of the property so Sue could put them in the ground and bring them to dazzlingly colorful life.

"They'll do well with proper watering," said Sue, adding that it should be done from underneath, not overhead.

"What do you think happens when it rains?" I asked.

"That doesn't count," Sue explained.

She also said that the peony I helped plant in front, where I had the tool mishap, needed to be transplanted to the back.

"It doesn't like where it is," Sue said.

"Did it tell you?" I wondered.

"Yes," Sue said, implying that she has more intelligent conversations with plants than she does with me.

So now I have to do more dirty work to make the peony happy. I hope the rake doesn't hit me in the head again.

"The Dish on Dishwashers"

Take it from a man with dishpan hands: One of the great mysteries of the universe doesn't involve flying saucers, although they are frequently spotted with coffee stains and break into tiny pieces if they fly off the kitchen counter.

No, the question that has baffled husbands for decades is this: If you have to wash the dishes before you put them in the dishwasher, why do you need a dishwasher?

The brilliant response, usually from the man's wife, is: "Because."

I may not be the chief cook in our house (Sue stands over a hot stove and prepares delicious meals daily, otherwise I would have starved to death long ago), but I am the chief bottle washer.

That's why I accepted the sad fact that we needed a new dishwasher.

Our old dishwasher was, without a doubt, the worst appliance ever made. It leaked so much that we had to put a towel in front of it to soak up all the water. I suggested that we could increase the value of our house by having an indoor swimming pool, but Sue nixed the idea because she would have to make dinner in scuba gear.

So we went shopping.

Our first stop was a home improvement store where we had bought not one but two refrigerators because both of our old units — one in the kitchen, the other in a storage area of the garage — conked out at the same time, probably from double pneumonia.

"Why," I asked Anita, the appliance specialist who sold us the two fridges, "am I supposed to wash the dishes before putting them in the dishwasher?"

"You don't have to," Anita replied, "but you should rinse them off or wipe them off if they still have food on them. Some people don't do that and let them sit in the sink for a couple of days. Then they have to wash them before putting them in the dishwasher."

"I wash the dishes in our house," I said. "And I have dishpan hands."

"Poor baby," Anita said sympathetically. "Maybe you should wear gloves."

"Is it true that men don't know how to load the dishwasher properly?" I wanted to know.

"That's what their wives say," Anita said.

"After Jerry puts the dishes in the dishwasher, I have to rearrange them," Sue said.

We thanked Anita and went to an appliance store that was having a sale.

"I'm looking for a white dishwasher," Sue told a salesman named Cirilo.

"We don't have any," he said, explaining that white dishwashers aren't in demand anymore. "You'll have to order one. And it costs a lot more than a stainless steel dishwasher, which is now in style."

"But stainless steel won't match the sink and the oven," Sue said.

"We're going to need a new sink," I chimed in, noting that ours is old, white, and chipped.

"They don't make sinks in white nowadays, either," Cirilo said.

"And we'll have to replace the faucet, which is old and gold," I went on. "So after this, we might as well get a stainless steel sink and faucet to match the dishwasher."

Sue raised her eyebrows in astonishment and declared, "For once in your life, you make sense."

So we bought a stainless steel dishwasher and called the A-Team — Anthony (our contractor) and Andy (plumber and handyman extraordinaire) — to install it.

"Do you guys do the dishes?" I asked.

"I'm single, so I have to," Andy said.

"My wife does the dishes, but sometimes I load the dishwasher," said Anthony. "And my wife will always say, 'You're not doing it right.' "

After he and Andy removed the old dishwasher, they put in the new one. As he was checking the hose under the sink, Anthony yelled, "Jerry! Quick! Turn off the water!"

I clutched my chest.

"Gotcha!" Anthony chortled.

There was no flood. And, after a test run, no leakage.

"I love my new dishwasher!" Sue exclaimed

"Make sure Jerry loads it the right way," Anthony told her. "And buy some gloves for his dishpan hands."

"Food for Naught"

Refrigerators leave me cold. That's because I can seldom find what I want to eat.

After moving around all the contents so I can locate the pickles or the pork chops or whatever I am looking for, I have to ask Sue where the heck (not my exact phrasing) that particular item is.

She will shake her head and say, "It's right in front of your nose."

As a guy with a prominent proboscis, I have often used this as a feeble excuse for my pathetic inability to find anything in the fridge. But she's always right. The pickles are right there on the second shelf, where even a person who is blindfolded, hooded, and wrapped in bandages can instantly locate them.

Sometimes, I think I need glasses — the prescription kind, not those that hold beer, which I could use after being baffled by the elusive food in my refrigerator.

So I went to my optometrist, Dr. Howard Weinberg, to see why I couldn't see.

"It's not your vision," he said. "You have a bigger problem."

I gulped and stammered, "What is it?"

"You're a guy," Dr. Weinberg responded. "I see it all the time," he added, asking me to pardon the expression. "Men can't find anything around the house. Your wife can tell you to go into a drawer for a screwdriver and it won't be there."

"I know exactly where to find a screwdriver," I said. "In the liquor cabinet."

"This is common in men," Dr. Weinberg said about our inability to locate things. "Every guy I talk with says the same thing."

"Can you find anything in your house?" I wondered.

"No," the doctor said. "And I wear glasses, so you'd think I would be able to see where stuff is. They don't help."

Dr. Weinberg's wife, Jill, the office manager, corroborated this alarming claim.

"It's not a vision problem, it's a man problem," she told me. "Even before looking in the closet or the refrigerator, they're asking where the thing is. They don't even try."

"My wife says the same about me," I told Jill.

"My husband is no better," she said. "And he's an eye doctor."

At least I found my car keys (they were in my right pocket, although I could have sworn I put them in the left one) so I could drive back to the house, which is filled with hidden treasures. A cabinet, a drawer, a closet, a room, you name the place, it contains stuff I can't put my finger on (I won't say which finger) even though Sue tells me the thing I am looking for — a roll of tape, a bag of popcorn, or, yes, a screwdriver — is definitely there.

Sometimes it is and I can't find it even though it's right in front of my nose. Other times it's not because Sue moved it and didn't tell me.

This is especially true of the food in the refrigerator. Compounding the problem is that we have two refrigerators, one in the kitchen and the other in the garage. Dollars to doughnuts, which I can't find, either, whatever I am looking for is in the other fridge.

Or it's in one of the freezers atop the refrigerators. I have to remove half the contents to find the sausage links (which, of course, are the missing links) that I want to cook with the eggs I plan to make for a big weekend breakfast.

When I take items out of the freezer, I sometimes fail to put all of them back, leaving at least one — frozen chicken, let's say, because we have more chicken than Colonel Sanders — on the counter, where it starts to thaw and drips all over the place.

Sue, miffed at my carelessness, will put it back in the freezer. Or she'll put it in the refrigerator, only to take it out again, cook it for dinner, and put the leftovers in the fridge.

"Where's the chicken?" I'll plead the next day while looking for something to eat.

Sue will shake her head and say, "It's right in front of your nose."

It's enough to make me rush back to the refrigerator for a beer. That's the one thing I can always find.

"Cause for Alarm"

The most alarming thing about being home alone, aside from being cast in a geezer version of the famous Macaulay Culkin movie, is setting off the house alarm and having to tell Sue, who left me home alone, that I could have been arrested for being in our own house.

That's exactly what happened when Sue went out of town for five days and left me — you guessed it — free to have a wild party that also could have gotten me arrested.

No, actually, I was all by myself the entire time, which would have been pretty boring if I hadn't accidentally set off the alarm on the first morning of Sue's absence.

After turning it off and putting a merciful stop to the shrieking godawful noise that I'm surprised Sue didn't hear from six hundred miles away, I convinced Heather, a nice and understanding person from the alarm company, not to send the cops.

"Everything is good," Heather assured me over the phone, though I had to ask her to repeat what she said because my ears were still ringing. "As long as you disarmed the alarm, you're OK."

"I'm home alone because my wife is out of town," I said. "She left me with a week's worth of leftovers to prevent me from starving to death or burning the house down."

"You'll survive," Heather said. "My husband is pretty dependent, too. He would eat at McDonald's every day. And he burns water."

"Has he ever set off the alarm in your house?" I asked.

"He doesn't touch it," Heather replied. "But if setting off the alarm is the worst thing you do while your wife is away, you're pretty good."

I thanked Heather for her help and for not getting me in trouble with the law. After hanging up, I surveyed my list of chores: clean the bathrooms, dust the furniture, vacuum the house, throw out the garbage, and water the plants.

I also had to heat up dinner every night, although I decided, on a rollicking Saturday evening, to send out for Chinese food. Afterward, I made microwave popcorn, which I munched while watching a movie on TV. Halfway through, I fell asleep.

Yes, I was a swinging bachelor. In fact, I spent part of one afternoon swinging in my hammock. But first, I went to the beverage warehouse to buy beer.

"My wife left me home alone," I told Paul, who rang up my purchase.

"Beer will help," he said.

"Has your wife ever left you home alone?" I inquired.

"My wife left me, period," Paul answered. "I'm divorced. I can go to sleep when I want, I can wake up when I want, and I can drink beer when I want."

"The first thing I did was set off the alarm," I said.

"At least you can tell your wife you didn't end up in jail," Paul said.

Arnie, the mailman, was sympathetic to my plight.

"I prefer being home alone," Arnie said as he handed me a bunch of bills. "I work on projects my wife didn't want me to work on."

"For me, a project is making coffee," I said. "And setting off the alarm."

"You're lucky the cops weren't called," Arnie said. "Enjoy your time off. And don't get in trouble."

Then I saw Mike, my next-door neighbor, who was outside with his wife, Corrie.

"How's Sue?" Mike asked.

"She's out of town," I replied. "She left me home alone. I hope you didn't hear the alarm. I accidentally set it off."

"I was away for a weekend recently," Corrie said.

"How did you do?" I asked Mike.

"Fine," he said. "I barbecued. I didn't burn the house down. And I didn't set off the alarm."

"Sue left me with food and instructions," I said.

"Not me," Corrie said. "I told Mike, 'You're on your own, buddy.' He did all right."

Ultimately, I did, too. When I picked up Sue at the airport, I told her about my adventures.

"At least," she said with a sigh, "I didn't have to bail you out of jail."

"An Open and Shut Case"

When one door closes, goes a new version of an old saying, the other one won't open.

For many years, that described the twin doors of my two-car garage, where I couldn't park even one car because of all the junk in there. But I did, depending on the weather, have snow, sleet, rain, and autumn leaves because one of the doors had a gap I could stick my empty head through.

Then there were critters, especially crickets, which sang for their supper while Sue and I were having ours. I'm surprised we didn't have a plague of locusts. Or a family of squirrels. They would have driven me more nuts than I already am.

The door that wouldn't open covered the half of the garage that the previous owner of our humble home used as a workshop. Since I am the least handyman in America, I turned it into a storage area where I don't store tools. But there is a refrigerator where I store beer.

The other door was off-kilter, kind of like me, which meant it could be opened and closed, but it had to be secured with a piece of wire that served as the world's most inefficient lock.

So Sue and I decided to get new garage doors.

This meant that half the garage had to be cleaned out.

The suburban renewal project included lugging a heavy bureau and a bulky cabinet out to the curb, as well as removing scores of other items that had been parked in the garage for no discernible reason aside from the highly questionable fact that we would one day need them. We never did.

Stuff belonging to our two grown daughters, both of whom have been out of the house since the administration of George W. Bush, also was in there.

On a sunny weekday morning, Jeff Ried and his apprentice, Mike Skuba, arrived to remove the old garage doors and install the new ones.

"Ninety percent of the people I see on this job can't fit a car in their garage," said Jeff.

"Can you fit a car in yours?" I asked.

"No," he replied.

"How about you?" I asked Mike.

"I live in an apartment," he said. "I don't have a garage."

It was a comfort, however small, knowing that ours wasn't so bad.

"One time, I found a suit of armor in somebody's garage," Jeff said. "In another one, there was a big bag of weed that the owner said belonged to his son. He screamed and said, 'I'm gonna kill that kid!' But the weirdest was this woman who hadn't opened her garage in about twenty years. She had three freezers full of dead animals. Her late husband was a taxidermist."

"Was her husband in there, too?" I inquired.

"Fortunately, he was not," Jeff said. "But there were deer and ducks. They were all petrified."

"The refrigerator in our storage area has a freezer," I said, "but it contains fish sticks and french fries."

"You're relatively normal," Jeff told me.

"Yes, relatively," I responded. "But thanks."

The first order of business was to dismantle the door on the storage side of the garage.

"It's called a dummy door," Jeff said.

"It could be named after me," I noted.

He politely didn't agree but could have when I asked if the door came in one piece.

"It wouldn't fit in the truck," Jeff said as he and Mike installed the new door, which came in four sections.

So did the new door on the other side. But first, the old, rickety one had to be taken off the track. Then, a new track had to be installed, followed by the new door.

I helped when I handed Jeff a box he couldn't reach.

"You saved me the trouble of walking all the way around," he said.

I also helped Mike clean up afterward by using a magnet with a long handle to pick up loose screws from the floor.

"I have a few loose screws myself," I said.

"I hope the magnet doesn't get stuck to your head," Mike said.

When the guys were finished, Sue and I marveled at how great our new garage doors looked.

"Now we don't have to worry about snow and critters getting in," I said.

"And one of these days," Sue added, "we might actually be able to get a car in here."

"I Married a Cover Girl"

I am not one to make blanket statements, but I will make one now: We have enough blankets in our house to cover the Green Bay Packers.

At last count, which entailed going to every room with a calculator (I could have used a pedometer, too), there were seventeen blankets scattered about the place. And that doesn't include the one in my car. Or the many that are hiding in closets. Or in drawers. Or even in bins I haven't looked in yet.

I did look inside an ottoman in the family room, where there are half a dozen blankets.

Then, of course, there are the bedroom blankets, but they don't count. Beds are supposed to have blankets. Rocking chairs aren't.

The only places in the house that don't have blankets are the three bathrooms. But that's only because they would end up clogging the toilets.

And I just remembered all the beach blankets we have. Frankie Avalon and Annette Funicello would be impressed.

Our house has to be the blanket capital of the United States because Sue is a bona fide cover girl.

"I like blankets," she explained.

It was the understatement of the century.

Sue not only buys blankets ("Is there a cover charge?" I once asked), she also makes them. And I must admit they're beautiful.

She gives some of them to our grandchildren, who order blankets from her like they were shopping on Amazon, except the kids get them for free.

Sue hasn't made a blanket for me, but if I keep complaining about all the ones that are taking over the house, I might be suffocated with — you guessed it — a blanket. But it won't be one that Sue made because she's too smart to leave evidence.

I can just envision the crime scene.

Cop (to Sue): "You say your husband smothered himself with a blanket last night?"

Sue: "Yes, officer. It must have ridden up over his face while he was sleeping."

Cop: "Why do you have extra blankets on the bed?"

Sue: "It was cold. And we like to save energy, so I got a second blanket for each of us."

Cop: "The one on your side is nice."

Sue (proudly): "I made it myself"

Cop: "Did your husband ever complain about all the blankets in the house?"

Sue (hesitating): "Uh, not that I can recall."

Cop (to first responders): "All right, let's get this guy out of here. Cover him up."

Sue: "Don't use a blanket. I'll have to wash it."

Keith Morrison would have a field day with this on "Dateline NBC," which Sue and I sometimes watch, although we regularly watch the various "FBI," "Chicago," and "Law & Order" shows, as well as movies and streaming series.

We do so while sitting in comfy chairs with our feet up and our legs covered by soft, cozy blankets. I will concede that they serve a purpose, which is to help me fall asleep before the closing credits, although if I have popcorn, Sue will warn me not to get buttery kernels on my blanket.

At least that won't happen with the blanket in the back seat of my car, which Sue put there in case we break down.

"It will keep us warm while we're waiting for a tow truck," she reasoned.

I haven't looked in Sue's car, but I bet there's a blanket in there, too.

We also have a lot of pillows, but not as many as our friends Hank and Angela Richert, who must have more pillows than any couple in America. Sue and I told them about all our blankets.

"You've got us beat," Angela said. "I may have to start a new collection."

Hank sighed and said, "Oh, no."

"Don't complain," I told him. "And be sure to sleep with one eye open."

"Here's Looking at You, Pal"

Mirror, mirror on the wall, who's the dumbest of them all?

The answer was painfully obvious — because I hit my thumb with a hammer — when I tried to hang a mirror on the family room wall.

The trouble began when Sue brought home a mirror she bought in a barn. Frankly, I didn't know barns had mirrors.

I can just imagine the conversation between tenants.

Cow (admiring herself in the mirror): "I'm looking a lot slimmer since I got milked this morning."

Bull (seeing his reflection): "And I'm looking like a real stud. I've got the horns for you, babe."

Cow: "You are so full of yourself."

The bovine couple must have mooooved out before Sue got there because the barn was occupied by humans selling antiques, crafts, and other items.

Sue brought home the wood-framed mirror with flowery side panels to replace a plain mirror that was hanging above the couch in the family room.

"This one is a lot nicer," Sue said about the new mirror, which is older than the old mirror." And I got it for only sixteen dollars."

"That reflects well on you," I said.

I noticed Sue rolling her eyes in the mirror.

I also noticed that we have a lot of mirrors in the house. The largest is in our bedroom. I can still recall the pain of hanging it when we moved in almost a quarter of a century ago. I'm surprised it didn't fall, break into a hundred pieces, leave shards of glass sticking out of my face, and bring me seven years' bad luck.

There's a smaller mirror in each of the other two bedrooms, which also have full-length mirrors on the backs of the doors.

The worst mirror is in our bathroom because I have to look in it to shave. It's a frightening sight so early in the morning.

The other two bathrooms also have mirrors. When I'm in there, which Sue insists is the majority of my waking time, I try to avoid my own gaze.

The most valuable (and coveted) mirror is on the top of Sue's dresser. It's a silver-handled hand mirror that her mother gave to her. Lilly is obsessed with it. She uses the mirror when she brushes her hair during visits to our house. Sue has promised to leave it to Lilly in her will.

I also have a hand mirror, but it has a black plastic handle and it didn't come from my father. In fact, I bought it at CVS. No one is obsessed with this mirror because: (a) it's cheap and crummy and (b) I use it when I trim my nose hair.

We have a mirror in each hallway, upstairs and downstairs, as well as four small mirrors in the living room.

There's also a mirror in the laundry room, where my dirty underwear and wet bath towels can be seen in the reflection.

But the main mirror is the antique that Sue bought in the barn.

Hanging it was a challenge because I couldn't get the hang of it. I had to stand on the couch, not an easy feat because my feet kept slipping between the cushions.

Then I had to nail a hook to the wall. Naturally, I dropped the nail behind the couch. Sue picked it up and handed it to me, whereupon I dropped the hook.

When I had both nail and hook back in hand, I came down with the hammer and promptly hit my thumb. My reaction could have shattered glass.

Finally, I got the hook up and tried to slip the mirror over it, but the sawtooth hanger on the back of the mirror was too narrow. So I had to use a pair of pliers to open the hook enough to hang the mirror on it.

"Great job!" Sue said when I stepped off the couch. "The mirror looks beautiful."

"And for once," I replied admiringly, "it's a nice reflection on me."

"Coming Clean About Vacuums"

I am not the kind of guy to sweep things under the rug. For one thing, my wife would lower the broom on me if I did. For another, we don't have too many rugs for me to sweep things under.

But it doesn't matter because I bought a new, lightweight, cordless vacuum cleaner that will help me avoid the toil and trouble caused by our old, bulky, asthmatic, and, let's face it, sadistic machine.

Not only did I frequently run over my foot while trying to maneuver the maddening contraption around tables and chairs, I nearly ruptured a vital organ while lugging it up to the second floor.

And on several frightening occasions, I almost tripped on the cord, fell down the stairs, and, yes, got swept under the rug.

The new vacuum is a breeze. I got sucked into buying it as a gift for Sue.

Originally she asked me for a Dustbuster, which would have been great for inhaling the popcorn I often drop in and around my not-so-easy chair, but Lauren suggested I get Sue a new vacuum instead.

Ever the romantic, I spared no expense (it was expensive) and bought it.

The machine is ostensibly for Sue, but it's really for me because vacuuming is one of the things I do to "help" around the house.

My job is now much easier because we have a new vinyl floor in the upstairs hallway, which previously was covered by an old, worn-out carpet that looked like it had been trampled by a herd of cattle.

And the stairs, which also had faded carpeting that I had to risk hospitalization to vacuum, are now bare and natural.

The work was done beautifully by our terrific contractor, Anthony Amini, owner of Performance Contracting and Management, and his talented assistant, Carlos Garcia.

"Vinyl flooring is the way to go," said Anthony, who had previously installed it in the kitchen, dining room, family room, and living room.

"Is that your vinyl answer?" I asked.

"You'll be floored to hear this," Anthony replied, "but yes."

"Are oak stairs a step up?" I wondered.

"They'll go down as a big improvement," Anthony said. "And they won't kill you because you don't have to vacuum them."

"I can't tell you the number of times I almost took a tumble with our old machine," I said. "The cord would get wrapped around my ankles like a boa constrictor and I could feel myself falling backward."

"I think the vacuum cleaner was out to get you," Anthony suggested. "The new one should be much safer."

"Do you have vinyl floors in your house?" I asked.

"Yes," Anthony said. "They're easy to keep clean. Dirt gets embedded in rugs and carpets."

"Is that the dirt on housekeeping?" I wondered.

"I'll come clean and say it is," Anthony responded.

When he and Carlos left after finishing the four-day job, I got out my trusty new machine and vacuumed the downstairs hallway, effortlessly going over both the vinyl flooring and the narrow rug. I did the same in the upstairs hallway.

With the antiquated apparatus, I had to bend over to adjust the height for bare floors after vacuuming a rug or a carpet. Now it's so easy — no adjustment, no hernia, no problem — that even a geezer like me can keep the floors clean.

All you have to do is shell out big bucks to buy your wife a brand-new vacuum cleaner that you are going to use anyway. And you don't even have to sweep your money under the rug.

"Little Kitchen of Horrors"

I could never be a herbivore, not just because I don't like vegetables, even though I am one, but because my name isn't Herb.

But there is a herb living in our house that I fear is about to turn into a carnivore. It is almost four feet tall, it stands menacingly next to my chair at the kitchen table, and it is probably waiting to eat me for dinner like Audrey II, the man-eating plant in "Little Shop of Horrors."

This one is a citronella, also known as the mosquito plant, so named because either it repels blood-sucking flies or, more worrisome, it likes to bite people.

So far, I haven't detected a mouthful of teeth, but that doesn't mean the jolly green giant can't ingest me in some other horrible way. I just hope I will prove to be as unappetizing to the plant as its yucky relatives are to me.

Sue, who loves vegetables and gets perverse pleasure in serving them to me, once asked if I like squash.

My response: "I'd rather play tennis."

So she went out to her garden, picked a big, fat zucchini, and served it to me for dinner.

It served me right.

Sue, who also loves flora (Flora and I are just good friends), has about two dozen houseplants. She waters them regularly and, obeying the instruction of botanists, talks to them. (The plants, not the botanists, who must be very lonely.)

"Talking to plants helps them grow and keeps them healthy," Sue told me.

"Am I supposed to talk to the citronella?" I asked. "It gives me the creeps."

That's because I can't sit down in the kitchen without practically being engulfed by the humongous herb, which is situated between my chair and a pair of French doors so it can get enough sunlight to grow even larger.

Whenever I want to sit down, I have to push the leafy layabout out of the way.

"Get lost!" I snapped as I sat down for lunch the other day.

"That's no way to talk to a plant," Sue said. "You'll make it sad."

"Do I have to apologize?" I asked. "The stupid thing doesn't even talk back."

"I can just imagine what it would say to you," Sue said.

It brings to mind (or what's left of it) the Oscar-winning song "Talk to the Animals" from the 1967 film "Dr. Dolittle." I hereby present my own composition, "Talk to the Vegetables," from a proposed movie starring me in the title role, "Dr. Donothing."

If I could talk to the vegetables, just imagine it.

Yelling at a head of broccoli.

Imagine talking to a turnip, chatting with a cabbage.

What a lousy dinner that would be.

The most demoralizing part is that Herbie II, as I have named the citronella, no doubt gets perverse pleasure, like Sue, in watching me eat greens that leave me green around the gills.

Also, the big guy has teamed with a poinsettia, which Sue has placed on a stool to my right, in surrounding me at the table.

"Christmas is over," I told Sue.

"It's still alive," she replied. "If you want to sit down, just push it out of the way."

Unless I want to starve to death, an appealing option if veggies are on the menu, I have to push both plants out of the way so I can sit down.

It reminds me of the lyrics to another song, "Stuck in the Middle With You," by Stealers Wheel:

Citronellas to the left of me, poinsettias to the right.

Here I am, stuck in the middle with you.

To add insult to injury (I stubbed my toe on the stool), after I eat, Sue wants me to push the plants back to their spots in front of the glass doors so they can sunbathe.

But there's good news: Now that it's spring, my plant pals will soon go outside, the citronella to the backyard and the poinsettia to the patio.

Then I won't have to talk to them anymore. And I can finally eat their yucky relatives in peace.

CHAPTER 3:
"MORE KID STUFF"

"Rub-a-Dub-Dub, One Kid in the Tub"

Of all the memorable things that happened during our granddaughters' first sleepover in two years — getting vanilla frosting all over the kitchen table after making cupcakes, almost freezing to death in an inflatable pool that promptly deflated, and eating charred popcorn while watching "Encanto" for the eighty-seventh time — the one that will go down in family history occurred when Sue had to sit on the bathroom floor with a glass of wine because one of the girls wouldn't get out of the tub.

Grandchildren can make you deliriously happy, as ours always do, but they can also drive you to drink. And not from a sippy cup.

"Lilly," Sue pleaded, "it's time to get out of the bathtub."

"I want to stay in, Nini," replied Lilly, who at nearly six years old is a pistol (in this case, a water pistol).

So Sue did the only thing a grandmother with melting patience could do: She went downstairs, poured herself a glass of wine, came back up, and sat on the bathroom floor with her much-needed sustenance while Lilly splashed, soaked, and sang until she was finally ready to emerge from the soapy tub and dry off.

Water dripped onto the tile. Fortunately, wine didn't.

Lilly and Chloe, who's nine, had been looking forward to the sleepover. So had Sue and I.

The girls arrived (with Guillaume) a little past noon. After scarfing down pizza for lunch, the first of our weekend activities commenced when Sue let Chloe do a load of laundry.

"Nini never lets me wash clothes," I said.

"Maybe you don't do it right, Poppie," Chloe suggested.

With Sue's guidance, Chloe did it perfectly.

She also did a great job of helping Sue make cupcakes (opening and closing the oven door was the extent of my assistance), after which they had to be frosted.

Here is where things got a tad messy. The frosting may have been the icing on the cupcakes, but it also managed (again, with my assistance) to get onto the tablecloth, which went directly into — that's right — another load of laundry.

Much of the creamy confection ended up on Lilly, who had it all over her hands, on her arm (she licked it off), and even in her hair.

"You need a bath," Sue declared.

Before that happened, however, the girls put on Sue's makeup, including lipstick and nail polish they applied themselves. It went beautifully with the frosting.

Then I joined them outside in the pool, which was filled with water so cold it could have caused coronary arrest in a walrus. Luckily for me, the pool had a leak, so we had to get out.

The swim was a lot faster than Lilly's bath, which turned out to be a marathon in which Sue washed the remainder of the frosting off the giggly girl but needed a cocktail to tide her over while Lilly created tides of her own.

After watching an animated show called "Veggie Tales in the City" (my fumbling with the remote prompted Lilly to ask, "You don't know how to work your own TV?") and eating hot dogs and hamburgers for dinner, we sat down for a viewing of the girls' favorite film, "Encanto," which I have probably seen more often than any adult in America. Putting a damper on the proceedings was the popcorn I burned to a crisp by leaving it in the microwave too long.

Halfway through the movie, the girls dozed off. Upon being roused, they went up to bed, putting the sleep in sleepover.

The next morning, they helped Sue make pancakes — with rainbow sprinkles! I must have eaten half a dozen of the heavy flapjacks. They are still in my digestive system.

After playing hopscotch, swinging in the hammock, and having a lunch consisting of chicken nuggets and leftover burgers, which now had the consistency of hockey pucks, it was time for the girls to go home.

"Lilly and I had been looking forward to this for years!" Chloe exclaimed.

"My friends' play dates aren't exciting at all, but this sleepover was the best!" Lilly chimed in.

After the girls and Guillaume left, Sue and I sat down to catch our breath and savor the memories of a wonderful weekend.

"Care for a glass of wine?" I asked.

"Yes," said Sue. "And I'm not drinking it in the bathroom."

"Math Confusion"

Here is today's test in basic arithmetic: If you had two grade-schoolers and one college graduate who happens to be the kids' grandfather, and you gave each of them a math quiz, how many would flunk?

Answer: One.

If, for extra credit, you guessed the dummy was me, go to the head of the class. I'll be up there, too, sitting in the corner and wearing a dunce cap.

It all added up to humiliation when Chloe and Lilly, who are in fourth grade and first grade, respectively, engaged me in a mathematical challenge after I took them off the school bus.

"How was your day?" I asked when we got in the house.

"Good," both girls responded.

"What did you do?" I inquired.

"Math," Chloe answered.

"Are you good at math?" I asked.

"My teacher says I'm a multiplication master," Chloe said proudly.

"That's very impressive," I said.

"Were you good at math when you were in school, Poppie?" Chloe asked.

"No," I confessed.

"Poppie was in school a long time ago," Lilly noted.

"I'm going to give you a math test," Chloe said. "What's eight times seven?"

I thought for a moment, then took out my phone.

"Who are you calling?" Chloe wondered.

Lilly saw what I was doing and shrieked, "He's using his calculator! You can't use your calculator, Poppie! That's cheating!"

"The answer is fifty-six," Chloe said.

"I knew that," I said feebly.

"No, you didn't," said Chloe. "How about nine times eight?"

"Don't use your calculator," Lilly commanded.

I hesitated while running the numbers through my head.

"Seventy-two," Chloe said.

"I guess I'm not a multiplication master," I said with a sigh. "Now I'll give you a test. What's ten times ten?"

"One hundred," Chloe answered instantly.

"I'm good in addition," Lilly said. "Ask me a question."

"What's five plus five?" I asked.

"That's easy," Lilly responded. "Ten."

"Here's a harder one," I said. "What's sixty plus eight?"

"Sixty-eight," said Lilly, adding: "That's how old you are, Poppie."

"Thanks for pointing that out," I said.

"Now I'll ask you a question," Lilly said. "What's three hundred plus three hundred?"

"More than I have in my bank account," I said.

"Did you become a writer because you can't do math?" Chloe wondered.

"Yes," I admitted.

"Does that mean you don't have to know anything?" Lilly asked.

"Not exactly," I responded, "but close."

I didn't tell the girls that when I was in high school, my worst subject was algebra. Here, as I dimly recall, which is how I recall most things these days, is the typical algebra problem:

"The Smiths are leaving New York for Boston at nine a.m. averaging fifty-five miles per hour. The Joneses are leaving Boston for New York at ten a.m. averaging fifty miles per hour. Question: At what point in the two-hundred-mile journey will they pass each other?"

Answer: WHO CARES?!

I once put that down on a test. I flunked.

When I got to college, I decided, for one semester, to major in business. In an economics class, the professor called on me and asked, "Mr. Zezima, what's the difference between macroeconomics and microeconomics?"

My answer: "The spelling."

I flunked that one, too.

Sue does the family banking. If it were left to me, we'd be in debtors' prison.

"Poppie, I give you an F-minus," Lilly said when class was dismissed.

Chloe was a little more charitable.

"You get an A for effort," she told me. "But if you want to be a multiplication master like me, you really need to do your math homework."

"In the Jurassic Dark"

When I was a kid, I knew all the dinosaurs — not personally, of course, because they were extinct by then and woolly mammoths roamed the earth. But I was a fan of such prehistoric stars as brontosaurus, tyrannosaurus, and especially Raquel Welch, who wore a cavewoman bikini in one of my favorite movies, "One Million Years B.C."

I have since gone in one era and out the other. Now there are more dinosaurs than I ever thought existed, my grandson knows every one of them, and he proved it by beating my old bones in a board game called Dinosaur Bingo.

It sounds redundant because geezers like me are considered dinosaurs by younger people (almost everyone else) and are supposed to play bingo and other geriatric games that don't require any real skill beyond the presence of a pulse.

But Xavier, who is almost six and wants to be a paleontologist when he grows up, loves Dinosaur Bingo. So do his three-year-old twin siblings, Zoe and Quinn, who are dino aficionados. All three kids have dinosaur-themed clothes, toys, books, pillows, backpacks, and lunch boxes and frequently watch TV shows featuring — you guessed it — Raquel Welch.

No, sorry, I mean dinosaurs.

In my youth, during the Boomer Epoch, behemoths such as allosaurus, ankylosaurus, brachiosaurus, diplodocus, stegosaurus, and triceratops were the most popular dinosaurs. Then there were flying reptiles like pteranodon and pterodactyl, pterrible ptitans from an ancient ptime.

But scientists have since discovered many other dinosaurs, some of them herbivores, which ate plants, and some of them carnivores, which didn't like vegetables and ate the herbivores. This is known as the "balance of nature."

Or it was until an asteroid hit Earth, wiped out the dinosaurs, and began the Age of Mammals. That includes humans. Males of the species invented beer, television, and professional football. Females of the species just ignore them.

But I am getting ahead of myself because of my humiliation at the hands of my grandson in Dinosaur Bingo.

"Let's play, Poppie!" Xavier said during a visit.

"How?" I asked as I looked at the cover of the box, which featured illustrations of herrerasaurus, maiasaura, ornithomimus, and other dinosaurs I had never heard of.

"It's simple," he replied. "You pick a card with a dinosaur on it and put it on a space on the board with a picture of the same dinosaur."

"What if you don't have a picture of the dinosaur on your board?" I wondered.

"Then you put the card in the box and wait until it's your turn again," Xavier said.

It sounded easy enough — for him, that is.

Because I had only two matching dinosaurs (centrosaurus, a

cousin twice removed of triceratops) and nodosaurus (the brother-in-law of ankylosaurus), and Xavier had a board full of matching dinos, including the winner (herrerasaurus, the shiftless uncle of T. rex), he breezed to victory in the first game.

Along the way, I learned that herrerasaurus had a big mouth.

"So do I," I said.

"That's because you're always telling jokes, Poppie," Xavier noted.

And pachycephalosaurus had a hard head.

"Me, too," I said. "Could I be Poppiecephalosaurus?"

"You're silly!" remarked Xavier, who also romped in the second game.

At least I learned about irritator ("the most irritating dinosaur," I surmised), fabrosaurus ("he must have been fabulous," I said), and therizinosaurus (which had such long claws that, I noted, "it could have used a manicure").

"Dinosaurs didn't get their nails done, Poppie," Xavier stated.

He should know, not just because he is already an expert in paleontology, but because he is a champ at Dinosaur Bingo.

The one thing he doesn't know is that my favorite prehistoric creature is still Raquel Welch.

"A Grand Decade"

On March 30, 2013, a date which will live in infancy, I became a grandfather.

I remember that day like it was yesterday, which is amazing since I can't remember where I put my house key, what I had for lunch, or whether I left the bathroom light on.

And that was today.

Still, I am deliriously happy to be celebrating ten years of grandparenthood.

In the past decade, Sue and I have welcomed five grandchildren, enough not only to count on the fingers of one hand but also to make a basketball team.

The problem is that the kids are better than I am in both math and hoops, although at my age, I am a better dribbler.

The oldest two, Chloe and Lilly, the daughters of Lauren and Guillaume, are sisters. Chloe is now ten and Lilly is six. The youngest three, Xavier, Zoe, and Quinn, the children of Katie and Dave, are siblings. Xavier just turned six. The twins, Zoe and Quinn, will turn four this summer.

If you think your kids grow up fast, wait until you have grandchildren.

I have often been asked if I spoil my grandchildren. The answer: No. That's my wife's job. My job is to corrupt them.

I take this responsibility very seriously, even though my antics with the kids can hardly be considered serious.

Making them laugh, especially at inopportune moments, is a specialty. Katie and Lauren, who must have haunting flashbacks to the days when I did this stuff with them, will simply roll their eyes, all the better not to see me doing incredibly silly things with their children, who have come to regard me as their favorite toy.

I have heard plenty of contemporaries say that the best thing about being a grandparent is that after spending time with the kids, you can give them back to their parents.

Not me. I don't want to give them back. I want to keep playing with them so we can continue having fun and I can then sleep so well that I won't get up three times in the middle of the night to visit the porcelain convenience.

The difference between children and grandchildren, aside from the spelling, is that your grandchildren are happy to be seen with you, whereas your children, when they were the same age, not only didn't want to be seen with you, they didn't want other people to know you even existed.

I love and am proud of my daughters, who have grown up to be great people and wonderful mothers. That's because they take after their mother.

Speaking of Sue, she is known to our grandchildren as Nini. I am Poppie.

When introducing myself to the kids' friends or the parents of their friends, as well as neighbors, teachers, and even complete strangers, I will smile broadly, extend my hand, and chirp, "Hi! I'm Poppie."

The kids will giggle appreciatively. Their mothers will practically suffer whiplash while looking away in total humiliation.

There are several important things I have learned in my first decade of having grandchildren.

The first is that mine are the smartest, funniest, happiest, most adorable, talented, fantastic, loving, beautiful (you get the idea) grandchildren who ever lived. It's just a fact. Accept it.

The second is that they come in handy for solving everyday problems, especially those that involve technology. Not long ago, Chloe and Lilly were visiting and asked me to turn on their favorite cartoon. I was fiddling with the three remotes it takes to find the right channel when Lilly looked at me in utter disbelief and said, "You don't know how to work your own TV?"

Then she grabbed a remote and instantly found the cartoon. I am thinking of hiring her as my IT person.

The most important thing about being a grandparent is that you should never turn down an opportunity to be with the kids and, especially, to do fun things with them. We've baked cupcakes, gone to the zoo, jumped on a trampoline, ridden on a carousel, gone out for ice cream, played board games, painted pictures, put on nail polish, blown bubbles, splashed in kiddie pools, attended dance recitals, gone to the beach, and done so much more.

Sue and I thank our daughters and sons-in-law, who have raised the kids with love and laughter, for letting us be such a big part of our grandchildren's lives.

It's been a decade I'll never forget. I just wish I could remember where I put my house key.

"Nothing but the Tooth"

I used to think that criminal possession of a forged instrument involved stealing a tuba. Now I know what I should have known for the past forty years: It's the act of writing a note to an unsuspecting child while pretending to be a fictional character.

That's why, in my latest act of forgery, I plead guilty to impersonating the Tooth Fairy.

I was pressed into conducting this shameful ruse when Xavier, who's six years old, lost his first tooth. Because Katie and Dave were out of town, and Sue and I were watching Xavier and his three-year-old twin siblings, Zoe and Quinn, for the weekend, I had to write a note from the Tooth Fairy congratulating the excited boy on his initial dental dropping.

Then I had to slip the note, along with the five bucks Katie had left for me, into a small canvas bag with a picture of a smiling, bowtie-wearing tooth on the front.

After the kids went to sleep, I put the bag under Xavier's pillow while he presumably dreamed of an overnight windfall from a winged pixie whose handwriting closely approximated that of his sneaky grandfather.

Against the advice of my attorney, who is in jail, I will admit that my career in forgery dates back to when Katie and Lauren were as young as my grandchildren are now. Under orders from Sue, who took care of everything else, I wrote notes from Santa Claus, the Easter Bunny, and, of course, the Tooth Fairy.

Naturally, the girls kept the notes, so I had to remember whose handwriting was from which character.

The Tooth Fairy's writing couldn't match that of Santa, whose writing couldn't match that of the Easter Bunny. And none could match mine, which ordinarily looks like the chicken scratch of a man whose hand was caught in a trash compactor.

Eventually, Katie and Lauren went from suspicion to the dismaying certainty that their father was a well-meaning but incompetent fraud.

I had been on probation for the past four decades until Xavier lost his first tooth, a lateral incisor in the bottom row.

The problem was that we couldn't find it. The tooth wasn't in his bed, in his pajamas, or on the bedroom floor. Sue suspected that he swallowed it. I told her that even though I am a devoted grandfather, following the tooth through his alimentary canal and into the toilet was out of the question.

I assured Xavier that the Tooth Fairy didn't need evidence that he had lost a tooth. And besides, what the hell was she supposed to do with it?

The next morning, the beaming boy ran up to me and said, "Guess what, Poppie! The Tooth Fairy came last night and left me five dollars! She also left me a note. Wanna read it?"

Since I'm old and forgot what I wrote, I said, "Of course!"

The note read: "Dear Xavier: Congratulations on losing your first tooth! I am so proud of you, and I loved coming to your house to leave this gift. Keep being a good boy and don't forget to brush your teeth every night before bed! Love, the Tooth Fairy"

Zoe, who initially said she was scared of the Tooth Fairy, saw the moola and said, "I can't wait to lose a tooth so the Tooth

Fairy can leave me some money!"

Quinn added, "Me, too! Then I'll be rich!"

It dawned on me that inflation had increased the Tooth Fairy's monetary gift from the twenty-five cents Katie and Lauren used to get to the five bucks Xavier received.

At least the Tooth Fairy still uses cash. What's next? A check? A credit card? Venmo?

But the most important question was asked by Zoe.

"Poppie," she said, "when your teeth fall out, will the Tooth Fairy leave you some money?"

"I hope so, sweetheart," I answered. "And she might even write me a nice note."

"Home Is Where the Art Is"

When I was in school, I was so bad in art that if I became a painter, I would starve to death because I couldn't even draw a good salary.

But my grandchildren are in school and they are so good in art that their works deserve to be in the Louvre Museum in Paris, the Metropolitan Museum of Art in New York City, and the National Gallery of Art in Washington, D.C.

Instead, they are in the Zezima Museum of Art and Snacks on Long Island, New York. It is an admittedly modest space devoted to the world's finest paintings, drawings, and illustrations, all done with brushes, crayons, and markers, all hanging on office, bedroom, and family room walls, as well as a refrigerator door, and all created by five talented artists ranging in age from ten to three.

These wunderkinds could, in my humble opinion, put Vincent van Gogh to shame, not just because each has an eye for beauty and a nose for trends, but because they all have both their ears.

I acknowledge that I don't know much about art, but I know what I like. It's the reason I have established Zezima's Two Rules of Modern Art.

Rule No. 1: If you see an artwork titled "Spring Butterfly," but it looks more like the grille of a '57 Chevy, don't buy it.

Rule No. 2: If an artist has been working on a piece for months and, when he's finally finished, calls it "Untitled," it means even he doesn't know what it is. Don't buy that one, either.

If my grandchildren's artwork were for sale, I would urge you to buy it, even though it is priceless and its estimated value is well beyond the ability of even the richest collectors to afford.

Besides, the kids would have to report their income to the IRS (Infantile Revenue Service) and they'd be legally obligated to pay more in taxes than they have in their piggy banks.

That is why I am humbled and gratified that all five of my grandchildren have recently made pictures just for me.

One, done by Chloe, who is ten, is a nine-by-twelve-inch masterpiece, ink on cardboard, its deep hues of blue, green, and yellow enhancing a playful drawing of her backyard, with a swing set and a slide meticulously done in black against an azure sky with a bright golden sun containing, in her distinctive handwriting, the beautiful words "to Poppie."

I couldn't be happier if I received a Monet or a Manet, which would be worth a lot of Money.

This magnificent piece, which could pair with van Gogh's "Starry Night," should be called "Sunny Day."

There's also a portrait of yours truly, with a mustache and a wide smile, which also was gifted to me by Chloe for my latest birthday. It features balloons with my age on them. The inscription reads: "69 years of being funny." Sorry, da Vinci, but "The Mona Lisa" has nothing on "The Mirthful Poppie."

Another work, done by Lilly, who is six, is titled "Wonder."

This pen-and-ink drawing lives up to its name, its deceptively simple lines showing an awestruck, long-haired girl, surrounded by stars, standing outside a house with another girl, smiling, in the doorway.

Imagine the price it would fetch in an auction at Christie's!

The youngest three grandchildren — Xavier, six, and his three-year-old twin siblings, Zoe and Quinn — are major talents in their own right and have gifted me with pieces done in crayon and felt-tipped marker. Some, from the twins, are even enhanced with colorful stickers, a bold statement that says, well, something.

Maybe that's why they are untitled. Still, they are beautiful, especially the series of floating hearts that express Xavier's feelings for me and mine, of course, for him.

In fact, I (heart) all five of my grandchildren, who also work in watercolors that sometimes spill onto the kitchen table. But that is a small price to pay for what critics would call true art.

I should take lessons from the kids. As Lilly told me recently, when I attempted a drawing of my own, "You really need to practice, Poppie."

Someday, one of my pieces will be good enough to hang in the Zezima Museum. I just hope the little artists will let me borrow their crayons.

"Not Exactly the Bee's Knees"

According to an old saying, which is reserved for old people like yours truly, the knees are the first things to go. That's not true for me because my brain went a long time ago.

But my knees are in painful pursuit because I injured one of them while giving horsey rides to my grandchildren.

It happened on the playground outside the school where Xavier was graduating from kindergarten. When I was his age, six and a half decades ago, we didn't graduate from kindergarten. We were just sent on to first grade with no pomp, circumstance, or — what I would have brought to the ceremony — whoopee cushions.

Still, I was proud of Xavier, who got the "Super Speller" award. In kindergarten, I could barely spell my own name, let alone "super."

Sue and I went to the playground with Xavier, who's six, and Zoe and Quinn, who will soon turn four.

Aside from equipment like slides and monkey bars, the two main features of the playground are: (a) children and (b) artificial turf.

And the children — not just my grandkids but some of their friends and even a couple of complete strangers — all wanted me to get down on my chapped hands and bare knees and give them horsey rides on the plastic grass.

The youngsters, who are wise beyond their years, pegged me as the back end of a nag. So they jumped on, one or two at a time, and yelled, "Giddy-up!"

I said neigh (I should have said nay) and clomped at a pace that would have elicited laughter from a snail before collapsing to catch my bad breath and await the next rider.

It was cruelty to animals. I'm lucky I wasn't shot and sent to the glue factory. But I kept going until I skinned my left knee so severely that it started to bleed.

"Poppie," Zoe exclaimed, "you need a Band-Aid!"

Quinn added sympathetically, "I want another ride!"

When we got back to their house, I asked Zoe where the Band-Aids were. She opened a closet door. I found a box of "PAW Patrol" Band-Aids with pictures of the doggie stars of the animated TV series.

When I put one of the colorful adhesive bandages on my

knee, Quinn shrieked, "Hey! You have to have an adult Band-Aid!"

"I like this one," I told him.

"Why?" he demanded.

"Because," I explained, "it makes my knee feel better. Am I an adult or a kid?"

"A kid!" Quinn replied.

"I skinned my knee when I was a little girl," Zoe said, "and by the time I was a big girl, it was all better."

I hadn't skinned my knee since I was a little boy. But my knees occasionally give me trouble, such as swelling, creaking, and throbbing for absolutely no reason, then feeling better the next day.

My right shoulder also gives me trouble from years of bench-pressing all five of my grandchildren, the oldest of whom is ten. I will lift them in stretched-out form and pretend to fly them through the air like a superhero.

I am convinced I have a torn rotator cuff, which sounds like it should be in a car instead of a geezer.

And don't even ask about my back, which I sometimes throw out. Unfortunately, the garbageman won't take it.

When Dave and I took Xavier and Quinn to get their teeth cleaned, the dentist spotted a small cut on Xavier's leg, washed it off, and put on an adult Band-Aid.

I pointed to my "PAW Patrol" Band-Aid. The dentist smiled and said, "Yours is better."

On the walk back to the house, Quinn challenged me to a foot race.

I grabbed my knee, howled in mock pain, and cried, "My boo-boo hurts!"

Quinn giggled and said, "You're a funny guy!"

"Are you going to give me a horsey ride?" I asked.

"No!" came the response. "You're too old."

It was, of course, a knee-jerk reaction.

"Funeral for a Fish"

Camilla Zezima sleeps with the fishes. Those eternal nappers include the first two Camillas and the countless other fish that have been part of our family, if only briefly, over the years.

Camilla III, as she (or he) was dubbed, lasted twelve months and was predeceased by the original Camilla, a female who went belly-up after only forty-eight hours, and her successor, Camilla II, a male who lived to the ripe old age of two.

The last two Camillas were gender-fluid because Chloe and Lilly, who talked me into getting the first Camilla, thought they were not only female, but the same fish.

Even I was confused.

After the latest Camilla joined his scaly relatives in Davy Jones's locker, I found out that Chloe and Lilly's pet fish, a blue betta named Igor, had kicked the water bucket for the sixth or seventh time. Lauren had lost count.

The kiddies apparently didn't notice the fish's lifeless body floating in his bowl and were none the wiser after Guillaume stopped at the pet store after work, got another Igor, and surreptitiously made the switch.

But I couldn't take that chance after finding Camilla III stone cold dead on the pink pebbles at the bottom of his bowl because Chloe and Lilly were coming over and I didn't want them to suffer the trauma they had escaped with their own fish.

So I went to the pet store and found a dead (or, rather, live) ringer for the first three Camillas.

"My pink betta fish died this morning and I need an exact duplicate before my granddaughters arrive," I told Meaghan, the fish department manager.

"People come in all the time with the same problem," she said. "They'll say, 'I need a red fish right away!' I'll take them over here, they'll get one and rush home. One woman had to replace a blue lobster, which is a crayfish, every other week because they kept dying. She had a two-year-old who would have been upset. She finally got it right."

I said I was looking for Camilla IV — "I've had to number them like the Super Bowl," I noted — and added that it didn't matter if the fish was male or female because the girls wouldn't notice anyway.

"It's pretty hard to tell," said Meaghan, who has four tanks at home. "I have about twenty fish overall," she added.

One of them is a betta named Sushi.

"He's going on his second birthday," Meaghan said. "My previous betta was Sashimi, who lived for a year and a half. The average life expectancy is about two, but they can live to four."

"Camilla III was only one, but he was going gray around the gills," I said.

"It's a sign of old age," Meaghan explained. "He may not have been new when you got him. This one," she said, referring to Camilla IV, who was swimming around in a little plastic container, "just came in, so he's young. He should last a while. And your granddaughters won't know the difference."

I thanked Meaghan, went to the checkout, paid $9.99 for a double-tail pink male betta, and headed home, where Sue and I had a solemn toilet-side service for Camilla III.

We tried to play Elton John's "Funeral for a Friend" on Alexa, but we would have had to pay for it, so we chose "A German Requiem" by Johannes Brahms, said a prayer, and flushed Camilla

III to kingdom come.

Then I dumped Camilla IV into his predecessor's bowl, which already had clean water. A little while later, Chloe and Lilly arrived. They fed the fish without giving it a second thought.

"When this one goes, "I told Sue, "we should invite Elton John to the funeral.

"The Early Bird Gets the Lemonade"

It may be true that time waits for no man, unless his watch has stopped, but it sure isn't true for any man — or woman — who attends a yard sale.

That's what I found out when Lauren had a sale that was supposed to begin at nine a.m. but which attracted a flock of time-ignorant early birds, the first of whom showed up at the ungodly hour of six fifty-two in the morning.

"Were they on Mountain Time?" I asked Lauren after Sue and I, who participated in the sale, arrived at eight o'clock, Eastern Time, to put out our stuff and have large doses of caffeine to wake up.

"I don't think they can read," replied Lauren, who put up large signs around her neighborhood and posted notices on social media advertising the sale, which clearly had the hours — nine a.m. to two p.m. — but didn't deter the crowd of bargain hunters who were roaming the yard when Sue and I showed up.

"Do you have any fishing equipment?" asked a gentleman who was angling for a deal.

"The only two things you need for a successful fishing outing are cold beer and straight hooks," I replied.

"Straight hooks?" the guy wondered.

"So the fish won't interrupt your beer drinking," I explained.

After he left, I made a mental note to have a cold one when the sale was over.

But that wouldn't happen for hours. In the meantime, I was the official greeter. This involved giving stupid answers to legitimate questions.

"How much are these baskets?" a woman asked.

"I don't know," I said. "I'm a basket case myself."

"We'll throw him in for free," Lauren told the woman, who smiled, politely declined, and said, "I have one like him at home."

Still, sales were brisk. Coats, shoes, knickknacks, jewelry, furniture, children's stuff, you name it, people were buying it.

So were dogs, including Tessie, a ten-year-old Shorkie who was there with her mommy and daddy.

"We have a rug she might like to sleep on," I told them. "And she won't mess it up because she must be housebroken by now."

I actually made the sale, though the rug went for only five dollars.

"You drive a hard bargain, Tessie," I said.

"Woof!" she responded enthusiastically.

The best and most consistent sales were made by Chloe and Lilly, who are ten and almost seven. They had a lemonade stand that Guillaume constructed. It was made of cardboard and had a roof, a sign, a side opening, a back door, and a sales window, outside of which was a table with plastic cups, paper straws, and a large jar of ice-cold lemonade.

"I used to drive lemons," I told one couple. "But as you can see," I added, pointing to sliced fruit floating in the yellow liquid, "these are real."

"Lemonade!" the girls shouted.

"How much?" countless customers asked.

"One dollar," answered Lilly, who took the money first, handed it to Chloe, and poured the refreshments from a spout.

Even people who didn't buy anything at the yard sale purchased the girls' lemonade.

"I work in a restaurant," one young woman remarked, "and they could have their own business."

The kids cleaned up, raking in fifty dollars.

The big winner was Lauren, who made three hundred and thirty-three dollars. Sue netted eighty-one dollars. I didn't make anything because I didn't bring anything of my own to sell. But the sale was a success despite the fact that I was the one who schmoozed with the customers.

When it was over, at two o'clock, it felt like five o'clock because of all the early birds.

After we cleared the yard of the stuff that didn't sell, I had the cold beer I had been waiting for since I talked with that fisherman hours before.

"You can't have any lemonade," Lilly informed me. "We sold it all."

"Rave Restaurant Review"

I seldom write restaurant reviews for the sound journalistic reason that I seldom go to restaurants. That's because I took a vow of poverty when I went into journalism and can't afford to eat out too often.

And whenever I do, it's usually in a place where the most difficult dining decision is whether to have french fries or onion rings.

But I am making an exception now because I just discovered a fantastic new eatery called Cafe Rio. In the interest of full disclosure, it is run by Chloe and Lilly, who are ten and almost seven years old. Lilly chose the name Cafe Rio for no discernible reason — a river does not run through it — but it sounds nice.

The girls operate the restaurant out of my house and rely on Lauren and Sue — and, if simple grilling is involved, me — to do the cooking.

The diners also have to buy all the food because the owners are too young to have jobs. Or at least jobs that pay money and don't violate child labor laws.

But their establishment is a culinary haven that I wouldn't hesitate to recommend to the public, except that the public isn't invited.

Here is the review:

CAFE RIO *(3 stars)*

If you enjoy burned hot dogs or greasy cheeseburgers served on fine china and eaten with glittery silverware, Cafe Rio is the place for you.

This fancy dining spot is unique for its ambience, which includes soothing music (provided by Alexa, the virtual assistant who operates on artificial intelligence, not a customer, because she can't eat) and a nautical theme (provided by Camilla the betta fish, who swims in a bowl on the liquor cabinet and is fed little food balls that are not, rest assured, on the human menu).

And what a menu it is! In addition to the aforementioned dogs and burgers, there are fries and broccoli, usually accompanied by a tossed salad served on the dinner plates instead of in separate bowls so the homemade dressing can mix with the meat juice, melted cheese, and condiments.

The resultant taste explosion tickles the palate!

But before you sit down to eat, you must make reservations to avoid being turned away at the door. (Actually, there is no door, although there is an entrance from the family room, which is often strewn with dolls, toys, and crayons and serves as the waiting area, to the dining room, where customers lucky enough to get in sit at a table with special place settings and talk, laugh, play word games, and, yes, even dine.)

You know you have come to the right place because signs spelling out "Cafe Rio," written on white printer paper and sometimes featuring stars, are taped to the wall. Accompanying arrows, artistically drawn, point you in the right direction.

The customers are greeted by the greeter (Chloe) and line up at a small table where the maitre darling (Lilly) asks if each diner has a reservation.

Their names ("Mommy," "Daddy," "Nini," and "Poppie") are crossed off the list and they are allowed to enter the establishment.

The table not only features name cards but is set with the grandmother's good china dishes and sparkling silver forks, knives, and spoons. Dinner napkins, slightly askew in the folding, are on the left. Plastic water goblets are on the right. Clear bottles filled with tap water (in place of their original contents: wine) are in the middle of the table, under a chandelier with bright little bulbs that illuminate the repast. The effect is dazzling.

The food itself, which may also include chicken, ribs, or pasta, is a bit spotty: excellent if prepared by the mother or the grandmother, not so great if grilled by the grandfather.

Dessert is a sweet treat, especially if it's cake or cookies made in the kitchen. Ice cream with rainbow sprinkles is also on the menu.

The owners' daddy, who is from France, has said that Michelin (the restaurant guide, not the tire company) would give Cafe Rio three stars, the highest rating.

This reviewer agrees. I just have to remember not to burn the hot dogs.

CHAPTER 4:
"IT'S A GUY THING"

"If the Pants Fit, Wear Them"

Even at my advanced age (approaching seven decades of decrepitude), I have kept my boyish figure. And I have always been stylish because my wife buys my clothes, which I sometimes stick in a drawer or hang in a closet and promptly forget about, only to discover them months later with the tags still attached.

But when it comes to pants, I have gone to waist.

That was shockingly obvious when Sue bought me two pairs of shorts that I not only couldn't button without exploding like the Hindenburg ("Oh, the obesity!"), but couldn't sit down in unless I wanted to sound like I was trying out for the Vienna Boys Choir.

"You're driving a wedgie between us," I said breathlessly.

"They don't fit," Sue acknowledged.

"They're size thirty-four, right?" I said.

"Yes," she replied.

"It's what I've always worn," I noted.

"True," said Sue. "But these are a 'slim' cut. You need the next size."

"Are you going to exchange them?" I asked.

"No," she said. "You're coming to the store with me."

Instead of "shop till you drop," I prefer to drop before I shop so I won't have to go to the store.

My idea of hell is being trapped in a fitting room as the door swings open and horrified shoppers witness the ghastly sight of me hopping around, with one leg stuck in a pair of "slim-cut" pants and the other flashing a glimpse of red, white, and blue underwear with hearts on them, two pairs of which I actually own.

Sue bought them for me.

This time I accompanied her so I could try on shorts that fit properly and wouldn't make me look like a total dweeb. Sadly, there was a "slim" chance of the latter because I was wearing dark socks, a wretchedly embarrassing fashion statement ("I'm a total dweeb!") that would never get me on the cover of GQ unless it stood for Geezers' Quarterly.

"Find a size thirty-six," Sue instructed as I looked through a pile of tan shorts.

When I found a pair, she said, "Now find one in navy blue."

"Now what?" I asked when I had unearthed a pair.

"Now," Sue answered, "go to the dressing room and try them on."

I opened the door, stepped inside, took off my size thirty-four jeans, and slipped into a pair of shorts, size thirty-six. I would say they fit like a glove, but they were more like a giant mitten with leg holes and a zipper.

When I opened the door and stepped out, Sue nodded and remarked, "They fit much better."

I got a second opinion from a sales associate named Sarah, who heartily concurred.

"You look like a size thirty-four," she said as she surveyed my midsection.

"Thank you," I responded. "I try to keep svelte. But why aren't there regular clothes anymore? Everything is 'slim.' I tried on a shirt a couple of years ago that was a 'slim' cut and I almost suffocated. I had to get an extra-large."

"That's the way clothes are made these days," Sarah explained. "They're all tailored for young people."

Sue asked if I wanted long pants. I got two pairs, "slim" cut, size thirty-six, and brought them to the dressing room.

I was in the middle of changing when my cellphone rang. It was a guy calling to remind me of an appointment the next day.

"I hope I'm not interrupting anything," he said.

"Not at all," I replied. "I'm just trying on pants."

There was a brief silence, followed by, "OK, see you tomorrow."

Then he hung up.

When I stepped out, the ladies signaled their approval.

"Men usually don't go shopping," Sarah said. "Their wives buy them clothes, the men try them on at home, the clothes don't fit, and they have to come in anyway."

"Like my husband," Sue added helpfully.

"Or," said Sarah, "they put them in a drawer or a closet and never wear them."

"Like my husband," Sue said again.

"I'm going to wear these clothes," I promised. "And no one will guess they're size thirty-six. I just have to remember to take the tags off."

"The Grandpa Grilling Club"

Like a lot of grandfathers, I have gas. That's because I recently filled the propane tank on my barbecue grill.

I have always been wary of the inflammable substance because it could, in addition to burning steaks to a crisp, blow me to smithereens. But Sue, who does all the indoor cooking, wanted me to barbecue some kielbasa.

More often than not, she wants me to grill vegetables, like squash, which I don't like. The only way to barbecue the stuff so it satisfies my discriminating tastes is to incinerate it.

I take greater care with my grandchildren's favorites, hamburgers and hot dogs.

Unfortunately, I haven't grilled for the kiddies in a long time. But since a visit to our house may happen soon, I want to be prepared.

So I called my longtime friends and fellow grandpas Hank Richert and Tim Lovelette for some grilling guidance.

"Get yourself a smoker," advised Hank. "And watch out for snakes."

Shortly after Hank and his wife, Angela, were married, they had a small gas grill. One day, Hank went out to the patio of their new house to cook burgers

"I took the cover off the grill and this gigantic black snake was coiled on the lid," Hank recalled. "Angela said she'd never seen me run so fast. The snake was harmless, but because it was so big and with the way it looked at me, I almost had a heart attack."

"Did you barbecue it?" I wondered.

"No," Hank said. "The snake took off, too."

Nowadays, Hank has a smoker on which he cooks brined chicken, ribs, steak, and, at Thanksgiving and Christmas, turkey.

"What about vegetables?" I asked.

"I'll grill potatoes, but that's it," Hank said.

"Does Angela barbecue, too?" I inquired.

"No," Hank said. "She's more than willing to let me do it."

Hank's best barbecue dish is the one Angela likes best:

brined salmon.

"She won't eat salmon anywhere else," Hank said proudly.

It's also the favorite barbecue dish of Hank and Angela's three-year-old granddaughter, Julia.

"She wasn't even two when she first tried it and she ate as much as she had ever eaten in her life," Hank reported.

"I bet Julia would like to see you on a TV cooking show," I said. "She'd be impressed."

"It takes a lot to impress kids these days," said Hank. "Unless I was a character on her favorite show, 'PAW Patrol.' "

"Your show could be called 'PA Patrol,' " I suggested. "But even if it doesn't happen, you can join my new organization, the Grandpa Grilling Club."

"We could have walkers with beverage holders," Hank said.

Since great (or perhaps warped) minds think alike, I heard something similar when I called Tim.

"It's amazing how much grandfathers rely on beer to get through the grilling season," said Tim, who has three grills: a pellet grill and a charcoal grill at home and a smoker at the family insurance business.

Tim and his wife, Jane, have six grandchildren ranging in age from fifteen to six.

"They mostly like hot dogs, but they'll eat other things," Tim said. "Jane grills, too, and has a great chicken wing recipe. If I'm making something the kids don't like, I tell them, 'Your grandmother cooked that.' It gets me off the hook."

The toughest barbecue sells for grandchildren, according to Tim, are seafood and vegetables.

"Kids don't like fish on the grill," he said, not realizing that Hank's granddaughter loves it. "And they hate vegetables. Who doesn't?"

"Our wives," I said.

"There's a way out of it," Tim said. "Bring all that stuff outside and then say, 'Oh, no! I dropped the vegetables in the grass.' To add drama, you can fall in the grass, too. Do that on a regular basis and your wife will have you looked at for physical problems. But the grandkids will love it. Small things amuse small minds. That's the whole point of being a grandfather."

"You've just gained acceptance in the Grandpa Grilling Club," I said.

"I wouldn't belong to any club that would have me as a member," Tim said, echoing a famous line by Groucho Marx. "But in this case, I'll make an exception. You bring the beer."

"Bye Bye Birdie Droppings"

My wife's car is for the birds. So I took it to a car wash.

Sue asked me to take care of business after a fouling flock that nests in a big oak whose branches overhang the driveway did its business all over her previously pristine vehicle.

That's how I ended up at Medford Car Wash, where I helped the conscientious crew clean Sue's car and got the drop on bird droppings.

I pulled up, got out of the car, and asked Abed, who was about to vacuum the seats and floor mats before sending Sue's sedan through the wash, if I could offer some assistance.

"This is my wife's car," I explained, "and I want to tell her that I actually helped clean it."

Abed smiled and handed me a hose so I could blow dirt, sand, and lint off one of the mats he had removed from the car.

"You're doing a good job," he said approvingly. "Your wife

will like it."

Inside, a very nice cashier named Nallely told me that husbands bring their wives' cars in all the time because they can't wash the cars themselves.

"Or," she added with a knowing grin, "because they don't want to."

After the car had come out the other side, I asked a personable crew member named Nikita if I could help hand-dry it.

"It would impress my wife," I said.

Nikita nodded and smiled. Then she gave me a towel and told me to see Taki, who was directing a couple of other guys on the crew.

"You want to help?" he asked.

"Yes," I said. "I'll put some elbow grease into it."

"Don't put grease on the car," said Taki, who let me dry part of the roof, as well as the left passenger door and the door frame.

"How did I do?" I wondered

"I'll give you a ten out of ten!" Taki gushed. "Five stars!"

Nikita was similarly impressed.

"Do you want your own car wash?" she asked.

"I could never do as good a job as you and your co-workers," I replied. "But if I did own one, I'd give you all raises."

Just then, Sam, the real owner, came over.

"Your crew is terrific," I said. "And I helped clean my wife's car."

"You could work here," said Sam, adding that his employees are, indeed, very good. He said he brings his wife's car in to be washed.

"You don't wash it yourself?" I asked

"No," Sam said. "But after fifteen years of marriage, she trusts me to make it look good. She had some dings and scratches. I compounded her car and it came out perfect."

"I've been married for forty-four years," I told Sam.

"I'm on wife number four," he said. "But she's the best one."

As he looked over Sue's car, he noticed some spots that hadn't quite come off.

"Do you have a tree next to the driveway?" he asked.

"Yes," I said.

"It's dripping sap on your wife's car," he said. "If you don't remove it right away, it will burn the car. But don't worry, I have some sap remover."

"I'm a sap," I said. "Will it work on me?"

"No," said Sam. "You're too big."

Then he noticed the faint residue of bird droppings that weren't fully washed off because they had been caked on the car.

"As soon as you see them, you have to hose them off," Sam said.

"The poop or the birds?" I wondered.

"Not the birds," he said. "That won't help you."

But the solvent solved the problem.

"Now the car is spotless," I said. "My wife will love it."

And indeed she did when I got home.

"My car hasn't been this clean since it left the dealership," Sue said.

"That's because I helped," I told her.

The next day, Sue spotted some spots on my car.

"Looks like the birds got it," she said.

"I can't wait until they fly south for the winter," I grumbled. "In the meantime, I guess I'll have to help clean it at the car wash."

"You've Still Got Mail"

I like to think outside the box, mainly because I can't fit inside the box. And even if I could, I would suffocate.

That's why I have never believed that the check is in the mail — unless it's one of the checks I have to write so I can pay all the bills that are delivered to my mailbox.

But I recently saved myself eighty dollars — the price of a new mailbox, which would have contained a bill for that amount from a home improvement store — by fixing a broken door on the decrepit mailbox that Sue and I have had since we moved into our house almost a quarter of a century ago.

For several months, the door had been unhinged, not unlike a certain homeowner. Every time I opened it, the stupid thing came off in my hands. I closed it by lining up the magnet on the door with the magnet on the frame.

One day the door blew off in a high wind. I found it down the street.

The mail was still in the box, but I couldn't take the chance that something important — a supermarket circular with coupons for beer — would blow away, too.

"I think we need a new mailbox," I told Sue.

"Can't you just fix the door?" she asked.

It was a good question with a bad answer: No.

So I sought advice from our mailman, Arnie.

"Bore a hole in the side of the mailbox and put a screw through until it attaches to the door," he suggested. "Do you have a screwdriver?"

"There's vodka and orange juice in the house," I replied.

"It might help," Arnie said.

"If I fix the door, will you stop delivering bills?" I wondered.

"Only if you put a lock on it," Arnie said.

Sue and I went to a home improvement store to look for screws — I couldn't find a lock — and went to an aisle with mailboxes.

"They cost eighty bucks!" Sue shrieked. "That's too expensive. We can save a lot of money if you do it yourself."

So I spoke with a helpful hardware man named Brian.

"Get screws that are an inch and a half long," he suggested after I showed him a photo of our mailbox. "If they're too short, bring them back."

Naturally, the screws were too short.

"Bring them back," said Sue.

That's when I met Chris, a hardware guy who had better advice.

"Get a threaded metal bar and a hacksaw," he said. "Measure the bar and cut it to the right length. Leave a little bit sticking out of the side of the mailbox, then put a washer and a nut on the end."

"It sounds too complicated just to get bills and junk mail," I said.

"You can do it," Chris assured me.

I bought a threaded metal bar, a packet of washers and one of nuts, and brought the whole kit and caboodle home.

I found a hacksaw in a toolbox in the shed, went to the garage to get a hammer and a nail, and walked outside to the mailbox.

When I tried to drive the nail through the side of the thick plastic box, the hammer ricocheted out of my hand and landed on the curb.

As this pathetic scene was unfolding, drivers were actually slowing down — some even stopped at the stop sign — to witness the witless.

Undeterred, I went back into the garage and found a drill. I put in a bit, got an extension cord, trudged outside again, and, like a dentist working on a stubborn molar, drilled a hole through the side of the box.

I slipped the bar through, attached it to the door, used the hacksaw to cut off the excess metal, and put on a washer and a nut.

It worked!

Sue was astonished.

"It's unbelievable!" she exclaimed. "You saved us eighty dollars."

Arnie the mailman was impressed, too.

"You did a good job," he told me. "Now I can't bring you a bill for a new mailbox."

"Eat, Drink and Be Married"

Love means never having to say you're sorry for taking your wife to a diner for your forty-fifth wedding anniversary.

So, sparing no expense for my beautiful bride, I took her to a pizza joint instead.

I admit that it wasn't as romantic as returning to Hawaii, where Sue and I honeymooned, or going back to Barbados, where we celebrated thirty years of wedded bliss.

But at least I didn't take my wife to the dump. That's where we spent our anniversary three years ago.

We had to get rid of some logs from a tree that had been

struck by lightning. It did not create sparks between us.

When Sue and I got to the landfill, I told the lady at the booth about our special day.

"It's our anniversary and we're spending it here," I said

"Well," she responded, "it's a unique way to celebrate."

We had so much fun that we made two trips. Later, we toasted each other with boxed wine.

This is the kind of exciting life that Sue and I have led since we were married on April 2, 1978.

It should come as no surprise to anyone who knows me and is willing to admit it, which narrows the field considerably, that I wanted to get married on April Fools' Day. But Sue nixed the idea, probably because she didn't want to get a whoopee cushion as a wedding gift.

Now, two children, five grandchildren, and millions of stupid jokes later, I can honestly say that if it weren't for Sue, I would be either dead or in prison. For putting up with me for so long, she deserves to be the first living person canonized by the Catholic Church. I deserve to be shot from a cannon.

So naturally, I wanted to do something nice for her on our forty-fifth anniversary.

"How about a ring?" I asked, noting that the traditional gift is sapphire.

"That's OK," Sue said sweetly. "Save your money."

"But you're priceless," I countered. "Besides, I found a blue stone in the backyard."

Sue smiled.

"How about going on a trip?" I asked.

"Where?" she wondered.

"Home Depot," I replied.

We have a bathroom project coming up, so it was an appropriate destination, even if they don't have postcards.

When we got back home, I told Sue I wanted to take her out for our anniversary, which was a couple of days away.

We don't go out to eat or even get takeout too often, but when we do, we patronize one of three places: the Chinese restaurant down the street, a nearby pizzeria, or, of course, the diner.

"We could get deluxe cheeseburgers with the works," I said.

"No," said Sue. "We should go someplace special."

We picked a new place that specializes in pizza but also has a menu featuring Italian dishes.

To prepare for the big event, I ironed a light blue, floral-patterned, long-sleeved shirt with a button-down collar and selected a nice pair of jeans and white sneakers, quite a change from my regular household ensemble of sweats and slippers.

"I'm getting dolled up just for you," I told Sue, who looked, as always, lovely.

After we arrived at the eatery, I informed Joey, our server, that it was our forty-fifth anniversary.

"Congratulations!" he said.

"My wife is a saint," I remarked.

"I can see why," Joey replied. "Would you like anything to drink?"

We each ordered a glass of wine.

"Happy anniversary!" Sue and I said to each other as we clinked glasses

When it came time to order, Sue picked chicken marsala and I showed off my sophisticated palate by getting spaghetti and meatballs.

"It beats burgers and fries," I noted.

Dinner was delicious. The bill came to $60.30.

"Thank you for taking me out for our forty-fifth anniversary," Sue said when we got home.

"You're very welcome," I responded with a kiss. "It was better than going to the dump."

"Bathroom Remodeling Is a Real Soap Opera"

Between long, daily, reservoir-draining showers to keep myself smelling fresh as a daisy, frequent shaving mishaps that draw enough blood to choke a vampire, and so many throne sittings that I could be a member of the royal family, you'd think I would be flush with excitement at the prospect of remodeling the bathroom.

But shopping for tile, a vanity, a toilet, and fixtures for the sink and shower has left me, if you will pardon the expression, drained.

The project became necessary after I took a shower and noticed that there was something wrong with the plumbing (the shower's, not mine). Specifically, the water kept dripping out of the shower head. No matter how hard I tried, I couldn't turn it off.

I didn't want to use brute strength because I don't have any. Also, I feared that I would cause a torrent to rival Niagara Falls, a tourist attraction that, unlike my bathroom, has postcards.

So Sue, who claims that I spend most of my waking hours in the porcelain convenience, told me to call a plumber.

I contacted our contractor, Anthony, who came over with Andy, a plumber who has done wonderful work for us before. Both are great and talented guys.

They agreed that because of leakage and aging, a remodeling was in order.

"For me?" I wondered.

Anthony shook his head and said, "You need to do something soon before you have more problems."

Thus did Sue and I embark on a search for new tile and all the other items that would make our bathroom a nice place to visit, even in the middle of the night.

On the first of so many trips to a home improvement store that we should have been given our own parking space, Sue and I were confronted with endless choices of tile, some for the shower, others for the floor.

And I learned a valuable lesson: When it comes to bathrooms, size doesn't matter. Even a small space like ours can't be remodeled without a large bottle of headache-alleviating pain reliever, which is kept in the vanity.

The question was: Should our new vanity be white or dark?

That conundrum was down on the list because first we had to pick tile. Should it be white in the shower and patterned on the floor? Or vice versa? Should we get subway tile for the shower? If so, would I have to spray it with graffiti? Should the floor tile be square? Rectangular? Hexagonal? How about a trapezoid? Should it be porcelain or matte? Who's Matt? Should we have a niche in the shower wall so we can store shampoo, conditioner, and fruity-scented body wash? Will picking a new sink give me a sinking feeling? Which fixtures should we get? Brushed nickel or chrome? Why shouldn't I take any brushed nickels? What about a toilet? Standard or fancy? In the end, who cares? Would a new mirror make me look any better while trimming my nose hair? Shower doors or a curtain? Would this be curtains for me? And, most important, how much of our liquid assets would go down the drain before all this was mercifully over?

Mitch, a friendly department manager who became our shopping adviser, was very helpful.

"This is more complicated than quantum physics," I grumbled.

"It's actually pretty simple," he assured me. "Your wife will make the final decisions. Husbands don't have much say in the matter. It takes the pressure off."

Mitch, a husband himself, was right. I've always believed that it's best for a guy to be like a bobblehead doll: You nod and you smile and you don't say anything.

We went through countless shower, floor, and vanity combinations, even taking individual pieces of tile home to envision how they would look in the bathroom, before Sue made up her mind.

I must say (I really don't have to, but just to be safe, I will) that she made all the right choices.

Now Anthony and Andy have to do the remodeling. When they're done, I'll invite the royal family to come over and sit on the throne.

"Air to a Fortune"

I'm probably putting my foot in my mouth for saying this, but Air Jordan, the fabulously successful sneaker line named after former basketball great Michael Jordan, may have to step aside for a new shoe, one named after a guy whose athletic exploits on the playground and the trampoline should be an inspiration to grandfathers everywhere.

I refer, of course, to Air Zezima.

I got the idea for my own sneaker line after watching "Air," a new movie about how Nike courted and ultimately won over the Jordan family by creating a shoe designed specifically for Michael, then a young hoop star who became a hardwood legend and, in part because of his sneaker, a cultural icon and a financial titan.

The driving force behind Michael's success was his mother, Deloris, played in the film by the fantastic Viola Davis. Deloris considered two other shoe companies, Adidas and Converse, before settling on long-shot Nike.

And — swoosh! — just like that, millions of dollars poured in.

If Michael's shoe, marketed largely to teens and twenty-somethings, could be that successful, why not a sneaker for geezers, the kind of guys who can't jump too high or run too fast anymore but who still chase their grandchildren all over the yard, the house, and the park without, let's hope, suffering pulled muscles, aching joints, or cardiac troubles?

I ran (actually, I walked) the idea past my mother, Rosina, who will be ninety-nine in November but is sharp as a tack, which distinguishes her from yours truly, and could probably talk Nike into designing a sneaker just for me.

"I'll broker a big deal for you," Mom promised.

I contacted John Donahoe, CEO of Nike, to tell him that I wear his company's sneakers and to ask if his design team could come up with a shoe for me, but I haven't heard back about my proposal.

Mr. Donahoe should know that Michael Jordan and I are on a first-name basis: I call him Michael and he doesn't know who the hell I am.

Aside from the lamentable fact that Michael is younger, richer, more talented, and better-looking than I am, we have something very important in common: We wear sneakers.

That's why I am the perfect person to join Michael in making oodles of money on our feet, which would prove that there's no business like shoe business.

First, my sneaker needs a good design, something appropriate for older men (and women) who are still active and hip, not inactive because they have broken their hips.

After much sole-searching, I have decided that the bottom of the shoe should be properly cushioned — with air, naturally — to give a bounce to our steps when we are running after the grandkids.

Also, the sneaker should be a high-top model to strengthen our ankles and prevent sprains when we are bouncing on trampolines, playing hopscotch, or dancing to music videos, as I have done many times with my grandchildren.

This design would also offer stability when carrying the kids or pushing them in strollers.

Finally, many children's sneakers have lights that flash when the kids move around. My sneaker would also have a first-alert system to notify authorities when we have stumbled and fallen while engaging in the aforementioned activities.

Safety first!

I am going with Air Zezima as the name, so the shoe won't be confused with Air Jordan. But since my grandchildren call me Poppie, I think Air Poppie is a possibility. Or even Air Grandpa. And for active older ladies, there would be Air Grandma. In Sue's case, it would be Air Nini.

I hope my brilliant idea leads not only to a new movie ("Airhead"), but to an endorsement by Michael Jordan and a lucrative contract with Nike.

As my mother will tell John Donahoe: "Just do it."

"House of the Rising Cost"

My mind is in the gutter. It's also in the kitchen, the bathroom, the garage, and all the other places where I have lost my mind in the twenty-five years since Sue and I became homeowners.

Now that we have been in our humble abode for a quarter of a century, during which time we have embarked on enough home improvement projects to bankrupt the U.S. Department of Housing and Urban Development, I can say with utter honesty and no small amount of pride that I am the least handy man in America. To me, a screwdriver is vodka and orange juice.

In spite of this shameful admission, or perhaps because of it, I pitched my own show to HGTV.

The premise of "House Blunders" is simple: An incompetent man (yours truly) tries his hand (which is holding a screwdriver) at projects that are well beyond his meager capabilities.

Lacking the requisite sledgehammer that many of the channel's stars routinely use to knock down walls and smash cabinets, the man and his much smarter and handier wife (Sue, a big HGTV fan) must employ professionals to undertake projects that would otherwise lead to the demise of the man in a ceiling collapse and sole ownership of the home for the woman.

Loren Ruch, senior vice president of production and development at HGTV, said my idea "sounds like a fun story." But "it's so crazy behind the scenes" and "we're just so slammed at the moment" that "unfortunately, I'm going to pass at this time."

Not one to give up easily (except when it comes to household projects), I am determined to mark twenty-five years of homeownership by passing along the following tips, observations, and other questionable knowledge.

The first is that you do not really own your home. The bank does. The legal proof is a document called a mortgage, which is what the bank requires you to pay so you can rent the home that the government says you own and makes you pay taxes on. You'd get a better deal from Vito Corleone, except he is a fictional character and, even worse, dead.

The second is that a house is not a home unless there is something to do. And there always is.

Over the past two and a half decades, Sue and I have spent tons of money on such things as: a kitchen renovation; two bathroom renovations; a new roof; new siding; new floors; a new oil tank; a new water heater; a new furnace; a new shed; new refrigerators, dishwashers, washing machines, and dryers; major plumbing and electrical work; foundation, wall, and ceiling repair; extensive painting projects; and new doors in the kitchen, family room, and garage.

And another bathroom renovation is underway.

Sue and I are fortunate to have found a great contractor, Anthony Amini, who does wonderful work at reasonable prices.

Here are some other things I have learned since we bought our house.

I am petrified of heights. I found this out when I had to climb to the top of the two-story Colonial to clean the gutters. Not wanting to slip, fall, and crash-land on terra firma, a Latin phrase meaning, "What you will be buried in if you fall off the roof," I got gutter guards.

A house is the perfect example of the law of physics, which states that any empty space will eventually be filled. This may explain why my office is so messy that the remains of Jimmy Hoffa could be in there.

Despite the work and the cost, Sue and I love our house. It's the only one we have ever owned. In response to real estate agents who are constantly calling to ask if we want to sell it, I say, "You'll have to drag my cold, dead body out of here."

Until then, I hope HGTV reconsiders my idea for a show. If it will help, I have a screwdriver.

"Martha and Me"

At my age (rapidly approaching a seventh decade of immaturity), I never thought I could be a swimsuit model, the mere sight of which would clear a beach faster than Jaws.

But then I saw Martha Stewart on the cover of the Sports Illustrated swimsuit issue, which I bought for strictly professional purposes, and realized you could be eighty-one, as Martha is, and still look fabulous.

Now I want to follow in her sandy footsteps and grace the cover of a major national magazine to prove that age doesn't necessarily go before beauty.

Even though I have maintained my boyish figure, I won't wear a bikini, as some of the SI models do. A Speedo would be more my speed.

"Let me tell you," Sue told me, "I'll never be seen in public with you in a Speedo."

It couldn't be any worse than my baggy swim trunks. They wouldn't get me on the cover of any publication except, possibly, GQ (Geezers' Quarterly).

I began my quest to be a famous cover boy by going straight to the source: Martha Stewart herself.

In an email to Martha, which I sent to her public relations agency, I wrote: "I think it's great that you are in this year's Sports Illustrated swimsuit issue. ... I would love to speak with you about what it takes to be a swimsuit model and if you think I could be one."

So far, I haven't heard back. I also left two unanswered phone messages.

"She's probably with Snoop Dogg," Sue said, referring Martha's rapper pal and business partner.

Undeterred, I wrote to MJ Day, editor-in-chief of Sports Illustrated Swimsuit.

After complimenting her on being age-inclusive in making Martha Stewart one of this year's models, I wrote: "As a guy who will turn the big 7-Oh in January, I would love to speak with you about what it takes to be a swimsuit model and if you would consider me for the next issue."

I haven't received a response, so I guess Ms. Day is relaxing on a beach somewhere with Martha and Snoop.

Next, I wrote to a publication that doesn't have a swimsuit

issue but is geared toward people my age and might put me on the cover: AARP The Magazine.

An editor there said I should go through the media office, but the contact person is on leave. Whether it's maternity, paternity, or Social Security, I don't know.

I made a final attempt with GQ (the real one), which usually puts young guys on the cover but might, in this enlightened age, be enlightened about age.

In an email to the publicity department, I offered to be a cover model, if not in a swimsuit, which would add a new wrinkle (or several) to the magazine, then at least in a tailored suit, which I would have to spend big bucks on.

No reply as yet.

So I went to a sporting goods store for a Speedo to see how I would look on a magazine cover.

When I told a sales associate named John about my plan to be the male Martha Stewart, he said, "You definitely could."

"I'll be seventy on my next birthday," I said.

"You look great," replied John, twenty-five, who politely did not add "for your age."

Then he handed me two Speedos, each a different size, and said I should go downstairs to the dressing room.

That's where I met Jess, another sales associate. I told her the whole story.

Jess, a very youthful-looking forty, smiled and said, "You've got it going on, Jerry."

I entered the dressing room and tried on both suits. The first, which I thought was my size, didn't go up past my knees. The second, which I thought would be too big, was so snug that I could have auditioned for the Vienna Boys Choir.

"Looks like I won't be a cover boy," I said as I handed the Speedos to Jess. "Maybe those baggy swim trunks are my speed after all."

"Bristle Boy Blue"

Picasso had his Blue Period. And now, I've had mine.

The difference between us — aside from the important fact that he had talent but is currently deceased — is that Picasso didn't paint his bathroom. I painted mine.

Or at least I painted part of it.

And I chose the color: serenata blue. It's AT-535 in the paint sample kit, which contains so many shades of so many colors that the kit could rival "Fifty Shades of Grey" for sheer thickness, though it's not as painful to read.

This was the first time in a decade that I've had a brush with disaster. In the first ten years of the quarter-century that Sue and I have owned our house, I had twenty painting projects.

The biggest ones, with and without help, were in three bathrooms, three bedrooms, the dining room, the family room, the very large living room (twice), and, worst of all, the hallway.

The problem with the hallway was that I didn't know where to stop. That's because it leads upstairs and connects to the hallway up there. So I ended up painting half the house.

The day after I finished, Sue said, "I don't like the color."

And she picked it out!

After that, I retired from painting.

"You're not retired," Sue told me. "You're just on hiatus."

She was right because a little over ten years ago, I came out of retirement, drove to Lauren and Guillaume's house, and helped paint Chloe's bedroom just before she was born. It came out great.

Even Sue thought so.

It eased the haunting flashbacks to my worst painting project: the kitchen of the condo where Sue and I lived before we moved into our house.

I was on a stepladder when I pulled one of two chains on the ceiling fan to turn on the light. A minute later, I smelled something burning. It was my hair, which had come in contact with a hot bulb.

I inadvertently pulled the other chain to turn off the light and the fan blades started whirling. They conked me on the head and propelled me forward. Paint splashed onto the wall. It came out pretty nice.

Still, Sue is a better painter than I am. And she usually picks better colors. But this time, for our bathroom, which was being remodeled, I chose a beautiful shade of blue, a cross between baby, pastel, and robin's egg, with a touch of sky thrown in.

"That's the one!" Sue exclaimed.

Our terrific contractor, Anthony Amini, whom we hired for the remodeling, agreed.

So did Anthony's assistant, the talented and versatile Carlos Garcia, who kindly let me help him paint.

"I picked out the color," I bragged.

"It's very nice," Carlos said. "I like it."

After he shook the can of paint and poured some into a container, he handed me a brush and said, "Let's see how you do."

I started in the corner and went from top to bottom, using the bristles to smooth out the paint without making Carlos bristle.

"Good job," he told me. "But watch out on top. Don't get any paint on the ceiling."

I stretched up and, in approximately the length of time it would take a tortoise to run the hundred-yard dash, carefully ran the brush across the top of the wall. Not a drop got on the ceiling.

"Do you want to use a roller on the rest of the wall?" Carlos asked.

"Sure," I said. "I'll be on a roll."

And I was, rocking the roller before handing it to Carlos to finish up.

"How bad a job did Jerry do?" Anthony asked. "Did he mess up? Do we have to paint all over again?"

"No," said Carlos. "He did great."

Sue stepped in and surveyed the paint job.

"The color is perfect!" she said approvingly.

"My Blue Period is over," I announced. "Picasso couldn't have done better."

"The Taming of the Screw"

You don't need a master's degree in nuclear engineering to put furniture together. But I'm glad my son-in-law Guillaume has one. Otherwise, I wouldn't have a nice new love seat and a set of matching chairs on the patio.

When it comes to home improvement, I am the epitome of DIY: Dimwitted Incompetent Yo-yo.

I have enough trouble putting together a coherent sentence let alone a love seat, or a chair, or a table, or a bookcase, or an entertainment center, or — God forbid — a gas grill.

Over the years, I have assembled all of those things with varying degrees of success and, often, injury. I once put together a plant stand that took me as long as it would take a kindergartner to read "War and Peace."

In Russian.

And printed instructions are no help. Trying to understand them fills my eyes with more glaze than a Christmas ham. I just look at the pictures, count the packaged pieces (screws, washers, and especially nuts, of which I am the biggest), and hope for the best.

I would have an easier time transcribing the Dead Sea Scrolls.

My worst experience was putting together a gas grill. It was the first one Sue and I owned and did not come already assembled. So, naturally, I had to do it.

The project lasted roughly a week, during which time I let loose with invectives of such hair-raising magnitude that the neighbors went inside and locked their doors.

When I was finished, there were pieces left over.

The first time I had to use the grill, I stepped back and asked Sue to push the button. I felt like a mobster who makes his wife start his car.

At least the grill didn't blow up. Fortunately, every subsequent one has come preassembled.

That sadly wasn't the case with the entertainment center that Sue and I once put together. Nothing tests a marriage like teaming up on a project that both of you are helpless to complete without scaring the wits out of the children and the family dog.

This latest do-it-yourself job — with the love seat and chairs — was necessary because the old patio furniture was either decrepit or broken. And I needed someplace to sit so I could drink beer.

Sue ordered a table that our contractor, Anthony, helped us put together, though not without a bit of frustration even on his part.

"This must have been made in China on a Friday afternoon at a quarter to five," he said.

Sue also ordered two chairs that Guillaume kindly came over and put together.

This time, she ordered a love seat and another chair.

When the items arrived, in two huge boxes, I asked the delivery guys if they had ever assembled furniture.

"No," said Orlando, the older one. "I think I could do it, but it's better to get somebody else."

Davy, the younger one, added, "I just deliver it."

So it was up to Guillaume — with my questionable help — to put the love seat and the chair together.

"No one deserves both the death penalty and the Nobel Prize more than the guy who designed this," Guillaume said while working on the love seat.

"He'd never get the electric chair," I noted, "because someone like me would have to put it together."

The most maddening part was tightening the screws with an Allen wrench, also called an Allen key or, more appropriately, a hex key.

"The long arm is too long and the short arm is too short," Guillaume said as his fingers turned purple. I'm surprised he didn't break a nail.

When the love seat was finished, I helped him with the chair by holding the frame and arms. My frame cramped and my arms ossified.

But it was worth the effort because the patio furniture looks beautiful. Now I can relax out there with a cold beer. And I don't need a master's degree in nuclear engineering to open the bottle.

"I Shopped and Didn't Drop"

If it weren't for my wife, I would have starved to death long ago. That's because Sue not only is an excellent cook who can make even vegetables appetizing (except squash, which should be squashed), but she does the food shopping.

But recently Sue was under the weather, so for only the second time in forty-five years of marriage, I had to do the weekly shopping myself.

As we stood in the kitchen, Sue went over the list of items she wanted me to buy. It looked like the battle plans for the invasion of Normandy.

Not only that, but she sent me to two supermarkets.

At first Sue said, "You can't handle more than one store."

She sounded like Jack Nicholson in "A Few Good Men." And I wasn't even one good man.

Then she reconsidered and said I could save money by going to the first supermarket for fruits and veggies, which were on sale, and to the second for other things, including milk, bread, lettuce, yogurt, frozen fruit bars, ice cream sandwiches, baked beans, crackers, and tomato juice.

Sue handed me the list, to which I added beer. She also gave me a circular, which was actually rectangular, with coupons that could be used in the second store.

"Do you have your assignment?" Sue asked.

"I think so," I answered tentatively.

"Good," she said. "Feel free to call if you need me."

As soon as I entered the first store, I was almost rear-ended by a speeding cart driven by a woman who blurted, "Sorry!"

She probably wasn't even insured.

I checked everything on the list — two red peppers, two green peppers, four peaches, four plums, bananas, scallions, and a quarter of a watermelon — and got them all except the scallions, which I couldn't find.

"They're on the other side," a nice lady told me when I

confessed to being lost.

"Men aren't supposed to ask for directions," I said.

"Your secret is safe with me," she said with a smile.

I had trouble opening the end of a clear plastic bag, so I wet my fingers and, muttering under my breath so fellow shoppers wouldn't call security, finally managed to pry it apart and stuff the scallions in.

Then I wheeled the whole kit and caboodle to the checkout, where I told the cashier that I was flying solo because my wife was sick.

"Don't worry," he said helpfully. "I'll bag the groceries for you."

"Thanks," I said. "I have to go to another store now."

"Good luck!" the cashier said.

The second supermarket was across the street, which is why Sue figured I could handle it.

I immediately encountered a fellow husband, about my age, pushing a cart.

"Are you shopping by yourself?" I inquired.

"Yes," he answered.

"Do you have a list?" I asked.

"No," he said. "I have to get only two items."

"Your wife trusts you?" I wondered.

"She has to," the guy replied. "She's outside in the car waiting for me."

After asking another woman for directions — I couldn't find the lettuce, which was in a case directly in front of me — I made the executive decision to get the frozen fruit bars and ice cream sandwiches last so they wouldn't melt before I was done.

It was a wise move considering that my excursion lasted about as long as the Super Bowl, commercials and halftime show included.

At the checkout, the shopper in front of me apologized for holding up the works while bagging and paying for her groceries.

"That's OK," I said. "I'm wondering if I got everything my wife wanted me to buy."

"Did she make a list and you're checking it twice?" the woman asked.

"I've checked it about twenty-seven times," I said.

When I got home, Sue said, "I was about to send out a search party. What took you so long?"

"I wanted to make sure I wouldn't have to call you every three minutes," I said.

"You didn't even call me once," she said with a smile. "And you got everything. You did a good job. I'm very proud of you."

"Jack Nicholson would be, too," I said. "The truth is, I handled two stores."

"And you bought yourself some beer," Sue said. "After all that, you deserve it."

CHAPTER 5:

"OUTSIDE CHANCES"

"The Strawberry Whisperer"

Whenever I pick strawberries — which I love because they are sweet, juicy, and a key ingredient in strawberry daiquiris — I become a basket case.

Even with a basket, which I need to hold the rich red fruit that inspired the psychedelic rock group Strawberry Alarm Clock (now I can't get "Incense and Peppermints" out of my head), I end up picking the sour cream of the crop.

That's why I relied on the kindness of strangers when Sue and I went strawberry picking at a sprawling farm that dwarfed the little strawberry patch that Sue has at home.

The last time we went strawberry picking was two years ago, with Chloe and Lilly, who proved to be so proficient at picking a peck of perfect produce that they put pathetic Poppie to shame.

This time, Sue and I went by ourselves. Without the expert guidance of giddy grandchildren, I needed help.

I got my first piece of advice from Jerry, the guy at the farm stand.

"Get a basket," he told me. "You don't want to carry all those strawberries in your hands."

"Will I get juiced?" I asked.

"You'll be a mess," replied Jerry, adding that I was the only other Jerry he had ever met.

"Jerry rhymes with berry," I pointed out. "Do you like strawberries?"

"Not really," said Jerry, who has been working at the farm for twenty years. "I'll have one here and there."

"There are lots of strawberries here," I said. "But if you have one there, bring a basket."

That's what Sue and I did when we went out into the field.

Sue took her basket and went on her berry way, leaving me to fend for myself. Fortunately, I met the Strawberry Whisperer, whose real name is Emily.

"You have your own basket," I said, noticing that she didn't get it from the farm stand.

"I've had this one for years," Emily said of her large white container, which had a handle and was stuffed with succulent strawberries. "It's personalized."

"In that case," I said, "you're just the person to give me some picking tips."

"You have to look underneath for ones that are hiding," said Emily, who pulled out a berry approximately the size — if not the color and shape — of a baseball.

"Mine are more like marbles," I said. "It's fitting because I lost my marbles."

Emily smiled, seemingly in agreement, and said, "I have to go now. Good luck."

I tramped through a row of berries, squishing some under my size-eleven sneakers, and met Mei, a young woman who was picking strawberries for the first time.

"You can use the ones you stepped on for strawberry jam," Mei suggested.

"I'm always in a jam," I said.

"You have to make the best of it," said Mei. "Just keep your fingers crossed."

"If I do that," I said, "it will be tough to pick strawberries."

Just then, and probably to Mei's relief, Sue caught up with me. She was carrying a basket that was bursting with berries.

"You're not doing such a good job," Sue said as she looked at my slim pickings.

She took me to an area where the berries were better and put some in my basket.

"You have to know where to look," Sue said. "You're too busy talking with people."

"One of them," I told her, "was the Strawberry Whisperer."

"Does she whisper to strawberries?" Sue wondered.

"Yes," I said. "And the strawberries whisper back."

"You've been out in the sun too long," Sue said.

We headed back to the stand with our overflowing baskets and saw Jerry again.

"How did we do?" I asked him.

"Pretty good," Jerry replied, adding that we owed fourteen dollars.

I handed him the cash and said, "When I get home, I'm going to whisper to my strawberries."

"Have a nice chat," Jerry said. "And enjoy your strawberry daiquiri."

"The Empty Nesters"

I'm for the birds. Unfortunately, they're not for me.

That was sadly evident after I took part in the Great Backyard Bird Count, a worldwide annual program in which gullible humans are tasked with counting the birds in their bathrooms.

Sorry, I mean their backyards.

After four days of looking up, which can lead to tree collisions and neck cramps, participants have to report the results via app or computer or, as I did, by returning bird counting packets to their local library.

This is all so scientists at places like the Cornell Lab of Ornithology and the National Audubon Society can find out why some avians are crazy enough to stick around and freeze their tail feathers off during the winter instead of flying first-class to Florida and getting their jollies by pooping on the cars of their fellow snowbirds.

The day after picking up my bird counting packet, I spotted a woodpecker pecking on a tree and wondered how much wood a woodpecker could peck if a woodpecker would just peck wood instead of trying to jackhammer my house, as many annoying members of their species have done over the years.

Unfortunately, I saw the redheaded rascal on a Thursday and the count was supposed to start the next day.

On Friday morning, I was up with the birds and — you guessed it — never saw even a single one the entire day.

Saturday, I was sure, would be better. It wasn't. Not a robin, crow, or any other kind of bird in sight.

Usually, they flock to my backyard like swallows to Capistrano, pigeons to Venice, or orioles to Baltimore.

I began to wonder if anyone had told the birds about the bird count.

I was getting desperate, so I dropped panko bread crumbs on the patio to lure hungry, unsuspecting, or just plain stupid birds. It didn't work.

Then I went to the shed to get a birdhouse. I leaned it against a tall oak and watched. Not a peep.

The Great Backyard Bird Count was at the halfway point and I was beginning to suspect that my fine feathered friends had gone into the Federal Witness Protection Program.

Finally, on Sunday, at eleven-fifteen a.m., I was upstairs when I heard Sue, who was downstairs, excitedly shout, "Hon, you got a bird!"

I rushed down and looked out the family room window to see a blue jay perched on a high branch of the aforementioned oak.

"Look," Sue said, pointing skyward, "there's another one."

I marked down two blue jays on the tally sheet of my bird counting packet.

As if a birdie board meeting had been called, a pair of cardinals showed up. I marked them down, too.

But as soon as I opened the door to step outside and get a better look, all four feathery visitors flew off.

"You scared them," said Sue, adding that the cardinals were, in her estimation, "a mommy and a daddy."

"Daddy cardinals are more colorful," I told her. "I might even say more beautiful."

"Like you?" replied Sue, who said, "We used to have a nice family of cardinals living in the backyard. I guess they moved, but I don't know where they went."

"Probably to St. Louis," I guessed.

"Why?" Sue asked.

"To join the St. Louis Cardinals," I said.

Sue looked like she wanted to peck my eyes out, so I didn't mention anything about the Toronto Blue Jays.

On Monday, the last day of the bird count, I was in the family room when I heard squawking. I looked out the window and saw five dark-colored birds having an argument. I don't know if they were blackbirds or cowbirds, but I do know that they must have seen me marking them down on my tally sheet because they immediately flitted away, mocking me as they went.

Thus ended the Great Backyard Bird Count. Final tally: nine birds and one flighty human.

The Audubon Society will know who's the biggest birdbrain.

"The Great Egg Mystery"

Why did the chicken cross the road? To lay an egg in my backyard.

That's the real answer to the age-old question. I know because the other side of the road is on my property, where a sneaky hen left her unhatched offspring and then, probably knowing that Sue planned to make chicken for dinner, flew the coop.

The fowl deed must have been done a day or two before Sue peered through a window, spotted something white a few feet from the back of the house, and thought it was a mushroom. But on going outside for an inspection, she made a startling discovery.

"There's an egg in the yard!" Sue shouted when she came back in.

I went out, saw the egg, and said, "What, no bacon?"

But the situation raised other questions: What animal laid it? How did the creature get over the fence? And, most pressing, would I have to sit on the egg to hatch it?

"It looks too big to have been laid by a robin or a crow," Sue said. "And it couldn't have fallen from a nest in a tree."

"Then it would be a scrambled egg," I noted.

"Cats come through the yard, but they don't lay eggs," Sue said.

"Not unless they're catbirds," I replied.

"Maybe it was a snake," Sue guessed.

It was a frightening possibility because a couple of weeks before, a fourteen-foot-long python was found dead on the side of a nearby road.

"It couldn't have been hitchhiking to get here," I said. "Snakes don't have thumbs."

Sue and I were baffled, so we took the egg to a veterinarian.

"It's a chicken egg," said the vet. "I'm surprised it wasn't eaten by a possum."

"If I saw one, I'd play dead," I said.

"Put the egg back in the yard," the vet recommended. "Maybe the chicken will return and hatch it."

"With the price of eggs these days," the vet's receptionist chimed in, "you should get her to lay more of them."

We now knew the answer to another age-old question: What came first, the chicken or the egg?

But there was an even more confusing conundrum: Whose bird was it?

Since chickens are fryers, not flyers, we suspected it came through the same gaps in the fence that are used by the aforementioned felines.

So I knocked on the doors of neighbors around back.

"No chickens here," said Bernie, who was babysitting for his newborn granddaughter. "Just a cat."

Trevor said his family has dogs but no chickens.

"If I see any, I'll let you know," he promised.

I asked Arnie, our mailman, if he knew of anyone on his appointed rounds who has chickens.

"Try a couple of streets over," Arnie said. "I hear chickens all the time."

At one house, I was greeted by Dudley the dog and his owner, John, a pleasant guy who said, "I've lived here for twenty years and have never seen a chicken. At least not one I didn't have for dinner."

Still, I found out that a lot of people have chickens.

A family that used to live on a nearby street had a rooster that would wake up the entire neighborhood at five o'clock every morning, but someone complained and the racket stopped. The annoying avian must have been adopted by Colonel Sanders.

My sister Susan's son Taylor and his wife, Carlin, watch their landlords' chickens when the landlords are away. And Carlin's mother and stepfather have chickens.

"The eggs are rich and wonderful," Susan said.

"Better than what you can get at the store," added my mother, Rosina.

Of course, there's always an exception.

My barber, Maria, told me that she and her husband, Carlos, had tenants who owned chickens.

"The eggs were delicious — except for one," Maria said. "I was baking and cracked an egg the tenants gave me. Whew!" she exclaimed. "It was rotten. Believe me, nothing smells worse. Now I buy my eggs at the supermarket."

Melissa, a receptionist where Sue gets her hair done, said she has chickens. When Sue showed her a picture of the egg in our yard, Melissa said, "It's been abandoned. You have a rogue chicken."

It never returned, so Sue took the egg inside and placed it in a plastic container that she put next to the furnace to keep it warm.

Nothing happened, so I took out the egg, placed it on a rug, and sat crossed-legged with the egg lying snuggly against my sweatpants.

"What are you doing?" Sue asked incredulously.

"Trying to hatch it," I answered. "I want to be a daddy hen."

That didn't work, either. Finally, Sue and I took the egg outside and cracked it, wondering if we would welcome a cute little chick into the world.

Instead, the yolk was on me. It was a regular egg, sunny-side up, like I eat for breakfast on Saturday mornings.

I didn't eat this one, but I did learn a valuable lesson:

When it comes to being a chicken detective, I'm just a dumb cluck.

"A Sod Story"

I have gone to seed. Unfortunately, so has my grass.

The problem is that it won't grow, especially in the front yard, where a giant oak tree throws shade at a lawn I have tried for years to make green and lush. Instead, I recently made myself green (with envy at my neighbors' lawns) and lush (because I gulped down a beer after a hot afternoon of getting down and dirty on a patch of earth that looks like it was manicured with a flamethrower).

Specifically, I dropped lots of "sun and shade" grass seed on areas of the yard where grass won't grow in either sun or shade. Sue, who has a green thumb (I told her to see a dermatologist), did the same in the backyard, which looks better but still has spots that resemble the shaved head of Curly of the Three Stooges.

"Soil will help," said Sue, who got some dirt from the pots of her potted plants, which were no longer in the pots.

"What happened to the plants?" I asked.

"They died," Sue answered.

Still, we spread the soil over several bare patches and covered it with blue grass seed.

"Maybe we'll get Kentucky bluegrass," I said, noting that we now had New York brown grass.

Then I filled a watering can with gin (no, I mean water) and sprinkled the soil and seeds. The next morning, I turned on the sprinklers, which did a better job. So did Mother Nature, who made it rain the following day.

Nonetheless, I was afraid that the grass wouldn't come up for weeks, if at all, keeping our property looking like the Death Valley of the neighborhood.

So I went to a home improvement store and spoke with a friendly manager named Casey, who suggested that I forget about natural grass and put down unnatural grass.

That's right: artificial turf.

"You won't have to water it and you won't have to cut it," he told me.

"Will I have to paint yard markers on it?" I asked.

"Only if you want to play football," Casey said.

I wasn't about to give up on growing grass, so I asked Casey what I should do.

"Put down lime," he suggested.

"Like the kind used in cocktails?" I asked.

"No," Casey replied. "But you might enjoy one after a day of yard work."

"What shouldn't I do?" I wondered.

"Don't spread fertilizer," Casey said.

"I've been known to spread fertilizer wherever I go," I admitted.

"I can see that," said Casey.

I told him that I have a lawn service, which hasn't been too successful in getting grass to grow, and that I also have a landscaper who has an easy job because there isn't much grass to cut.

"I keep getting conflicting advice," I said. "I don't know when to drop seed, when to water, or when to spread fertilizer. Now I don't even know when to put lime in my cocktails."

"You can drop seed anytime," Casey said. "And you should water the grass every day."

"What about cocktails?" I asked.

"Wait until five o'clock," Casey said.

A few days later, I was visited by Wayne, from the lawn service, who told me it's best to drop seed in the fall and that I should water the grass only twice a week.

"Otherwise," he said, "you'll overwater and weeds will grow. You don't want to feed the weed."

Wayne had come by to put down weed killer but said he wouldn't do that because he saw that I had already dropped seed and the weed killer would also kill the new grass.

"Instead, I'll spread fertilizer," he said.

"I thought fertilizing in the spring was bad," I said.

"It is," Wayne replied. "But I'm using starter fertilizer."

"Is there finishing fertilizer?" I wondered.

"Yes," said Wayne. "It's used in the fall."

Disregarding all advice, Sue and I have been faithfully watering the seeds every day and running the sprinklers every other day. Miraculously, little green blades are coming up.

"Looks like we won't have to get artificial turf," I said. "But trying to improve our lawn is a pain in the grass."

"The Garden of Eatin' "

My wife has ants in her plants. She also has rabbits and squirrels and birds, oh, my!

These creatures have been eating the vegetables in Sue's garden. In retaliation, my green-thumbed sweetheart has been waging a constant battle to stop the pesky invaders from decimating the fruits of her labors.

"They're destroying my zucchini!" Sue moaned after discovering that some creepy critters had been gorging on the thick courgettes that she takes supreme pleasure in making me eat.

To put it mildly, I am not a fan of squash, although I do like tennis. Sue is also growing cucumbers, which I hate, too, so it's a good thing I don't play pickleball.

Anyway, she is at her wit's end with these creatures. (With me, she is only at her half-wit's end.)

The question is: How do we get rid of them?

Answer: Dynamite.

As an animal lover, I don't suggest harming the fine feathered, feelered, and furry friends that are feasting and fattening in a feeding frenzy.

Instead, I think the explosives should be used on the veggies themselves. Or maybe a controlled burn would do the trick, though with my luck it would burn out of control, spread to the house, and incinerate all the really good and healthful stuff I love to eat, like Twinkies and beef jerky.

I admit that this is a garden-variety problem, but it really bugs (we have plenty of them as well) the dedicated people, like Sue, who grow things that their otherwise appreciative spouses, like me, can't stand.

That's why I really shouldn't complain that an unidentified rodent has been nibbling at the broccoli. If I could talk to the animals — a bunny would probably respond by asking me what's up — I would encourage them to wolf down every last head, stalk, and leaf popping up out of our small patch of earth.

I would also politely ask them to lay off the crops I actually like, such as tomatoes, string beans, and eggplant.

Then there are the herbs: Herb Alpert, Herb Brooks, and Herb Shriner. No, sorry, I mean parsley, sage, rosemary, and thyme, which Sue is growing, though not to the tune of "Scarborough Fair."

Now you may be thinking: This is nature, you idiot! And the animals were here first.

I beg to differ. Sue and I have lived in our house — and on our property, including the garden — for twenty-five years. No ant, rabbit, squirrel, or bird lives that long. So we were here first.

I have proof. It's called a mortgage. Maybe I should charge the critters rent for taking up residence on our grounds. Sometimes the smaller ones, like flies and bees, get into the house. When I tell them to buzz off, they don't listen. It's maddening.

So Sue has resorted to using a spray that supposedly repels vermin. (I'm surprised she hasn't used it on me.)

There are many such products on the market, all claiming to get rid of garden pests without poisoning them. And therein lies the problem: They don't work.

This has spawned lots of do-it-yourself remedies. Some gardeners swear by a mixture of water and hot red pepper, then swear at the solution because it turns out to be no solution at all.

I would opt for beer, just to get the little critters stinking drunk, but why waste my supply?

Of course, I could put up a scarecrow with my photo on the face, but that would be cruelty to animals.

In the end, gardeners like Sue must learn to live in harmony with God's creatures. And I think they should eat all the zucchini they damn well please.

CHAPTER 6:

"DIAL 'M' FOR MADNESS"

"Warranty Calls Are an Auto Motive"

The main difference between me and my car — aside from the alarming fact that my fluids need to be changed twice a night — is that I don't come with an extended warranty.

But I am expecting to get a phone call about the coverage on my brand-new vehicle any minute now.

That's because the last time I bought a car, a couple of years ago on a trade-in, I got a call from a warranty salesperson — this is absolutely true — the day after I drove the vehicle home.

Here is roughly how the conversation went.

Me: "Hello?"

Salesperson: "We've been trying to reach you about your car's extended warranty."

Me: "Why? I just got the car!"

Salesperson: "What is the make and model of your vehicle?"

Me: "I'll answer that if you can tell me my name."

Salesperson: "We are not allowed to give out that information, sir."

Me: "You called me, so you have to know who I am. You can't tell me my own name?"

Salesperson: "No, sir."

Me: "Is this some kind of scam?"

Salesperson: (Click)

I have been expecting a similar call, scores of which I have received since I got my previous car, now that I have a new set of wheels.

But I am relieved to know I am not the only person whose car warranty is of great concern to the nice, if persistent, folks who care deeply about my car's longevity.

Sue, whose vehicle is still under warranty, gets these calls, too.

So do the employees of the car dealership, Hyundai 112 in Medford, New York.

"Isn't it amazing?" said sales representative James Boyd, a great guy who has helped me and Sue through several automotive transactions. "They call me, too."

They also call sales manager Austin Malkasian, who said, "I'm surprised there aren't notes in candy bars about car warranties. I saw a meme showing a guy picking up a bottle that had washed up on a beach. The bottle had a scroll inside saying, 'We've been trying to reach you about your car's extended warranty.' "

Sales producer Jim Maxent said, "One time I got a warranty call. The person asked, 'What's the make and model of your car?' I replied, 'I have a 1972 Plymouth Fury with 750,000 miles on it.' They hung up."

Said business manager Allison Rollero, "I tell them I don't even have a car."

General manager Greg Galardi said, "I'm surprised you didn't get a call ten minutes before you actually bought the car. That's probably what it will come to one of these days."

But that didn't deter me from trading in my "old" car, which had only seventeen thousand miles on it, for a vehicle so new that its official release date is next year.

"The car I had before the car I am trading in now had twenty-six thousand miles on it," I told James. "The mileage gets less every time. Does this mean I'll get another trade-in deal next month?"

"No," said James "But that doesn't mean you won't get calls about the new car's warranty."

James added that he once got a call from the daughter of an elderly customer who had fallen for the warranty scheme.

"This guy didn't want to pay a penny extra for anything, but he fell for the scam," James said. "So now he was paying an extra hundred dollars a month. When his daughter called, I told her that he already had a warranty."

"Do I have a warranty?" I asked.

"Yes," said James. "It's five years, sixty thousand miles. And you get a ten-year, one-hundred-thousand-mile powertrain warranty."

"Powertrain?" I asked. "I'm not buying a locomotive, am I?"

"No," James assured me. "But the warranty is for longer than you'll have the car."

I thanked James and fellow sales rep Manny Gomez for hooking up the Apple CarPlay, because men are prohibited by federal law from asking for directions, and said I was very happy with my new car.

"I'm glad," said James. "But don't be surprised if you get a warranty call while you're driving home."

"Hack to the Future"

At the risk of plagiarizing Popeye, who is a cartoon character and can't sue me, I am what I am. I can't say what I am in polite company, but I can say who I am: a guy nobody should want to be because, on most days, I don't want to be myself.

But that hasn't stopped some people — I don't know who they are — from wanting to be me and trying to accomplish such a dubious feat by stealing my identity.

I may be a mild-mannered reporter for a great metropolitan newspaper, but I don't have a secret identity for the following reasons:

(a) I can't fly, which is a good thing because I'm afraid of heights.

(b) I'm not faster than a speeding bullet, except when I'm rushing to the refrigerator for a beer.

(c) I don't wear tights and a cape. Well, at least not during the week. What I do on weekends is nobody's business.

My real identity is so pathetic that no one in his right mind should want to steal it. And if the perpetrator is caught, he could avoid conviction by pleading insanity.

Still, I have been the subject of some recent hack attempts on social media by individuals I can only describe as — that's right! — hacks.

One claiming to be me asked my friends to become his friends, which prompted me to issue the following warning: "I've been hacked. Why anybody would want to be me is an enduring mystery. I don't want to be myself, but it's too late to do anything about it. Anyway, do not accept a friend request from anyone purporting to be yours truly. Sorry for the inconvenience."

My sister Elizabeth responded: "I'm anxious to see if the new Jerry Z is going to pay your bills and take care of your yard. In which case stolen identity pays!"

Daniel wrote: "That wasn't you naked with a bowl of fruit on your head?"

I replied: "I ate the fruit. The rest is true."

Rick A. wrote: "You mean I should disregard the message that you're holding $1,432,679 for me and all I have to do is send you $2,000 as a good faith measure???"

Rick L. wrote: "Can't imagine you had that many friends to begin with."

More recently, there was another attempt to bamboozle friends who were already my friends into becoming my friends again. The message read: "Jerry Xezima sent you a friend request."

I immediately posted this warning: "X marks the spot where I have been hacked by someone claiming to be Jerry Xezima. It's not me (why anyone would want to be, I don't know), so please do not accept the friend request."

This sparked a volley of responses.

Jim: "I think Jerry Zezima has been hacked, or else he's the new premier of China."

Dan: "I got that, and one from Jerry Eczema, but I think a cream makes that one goes away."

Robin L.: "That wasn't you messaging me about my car insurance?"

The worst part of this whole thing has been trying to prove I'm me. That's what I had to do for the IRS on a website called ID.me, an online identity network that allows people to prove they are who they say they are.

I needed my Social Security card, my driver's license, and my cable bill. Then I had to choose a new password because I forgot my old password, one of approximately one hundred and fifty passwords I have just so I can prove I am, for better or for worse, Jerry Zezima.

Next I had to go on a video call and be interviewed by a "conference host" who was not, of course, identified. After that, I had to take a selfie for facial recognition.

Finally, I needed a "verification partner." I chose Sue, who verified my identity and added, "Believe me, there's no one else like him."

Remember that the next time you get a friend request.

"Headed Off at the Password"

I'm a mild and lazy guy. That's the only reason I haven't been driven stark, raving mad by an evil cabal I am convinced is now running my life and has turned it into one big gaslight job.

There is no other explanation for the fact that every business, organization, outlet, entity, agency, or group I must deal with requires me to have a username and a password that don't work and must be changed every damn time I try to log in to one of their websites.

I envision shadowy figures in a small room ringed with screens that show me on my computer, attempting to pay a loan or trying to get the information I need to meet my obligations and stay out of either jail or, more likely, the loony bin.

"Look," chortles the ringleader, "he's banging his fist on the desk and cursing a blue streak because he can't log in!"

"Let's make sure his password doesn't work!" a henchman chimes in.

"How about his username?" another one asks.

"We'll force him to come up with a new one!" a lieutenant says gleefully.

"And that won't work, either!" says a fellow fiend.

"Brilliant!" they all agree.

"And when he calls for assistance," the ringleader sneers, "he'll be put on hold for an eternity. Ha ha ha ha ha!"

It just so happens that I did call for assistance recently after being rebuffed in my several maddening attempts to log in to a website so I could find out when the next loan payment is due and whether I could get an extension.

"I apologize for the inconvenience," a very nice customer care representative named Darlene said when I finally got through. "More than likely, you tried to log in to the old website."

"Is there a new website?" I wondered.

"We have old and new systems in place," Darlene answered. "I know it's a big headache."

"At this point," I said, "the ache is in a lower portion of my anatomy."

Darlene chuckled and said, "I hear you." Then she added, "Go to the new website and log in."

"My username doesn't work," I said when I tried. "I got a new username last week after being told that the one I had before was no good."

"What happened?" Darlene asked.

"The new username did, indeed, work," I said. "But when I went back on the website, it didn't work anymore. So I had to use the old one."

"Did it work?" Darlene inquired.

"Yes," I said. "But it doesn't work now."

"What do you see on your screen?" Darlene asked.

"It says, 'We're sorry. We can't find the User ID and Password combination you entered. Remember, your Password is case sensitive. Please go to Forgot User ID or Forgot Password, or try to log in again,' " I told her.

Darlene said I should use the new-old username. Or the old-new one. By that time, I was totally confused. But at least it worked. Unfortunately, what I thought was my password didn't. So Darlene texted me a new, temporary password that looked like the electron configuration for boron.

"You can change it to whatever you want," she said. "But

don't use your previous password."

"I can't remember what the hell it was anyway," I confessed.

I chose a password that was no good because it wasn't alphameric, a term that encompasses letters and numerals but not certain symbols. I was disappointed since I would have chosen a raised-finger emoji.

So I picked an acceptable password and, utilizing my sophisticated filing system, wrote it down on a Post-it Note.

I ignored a box that allowed me to write a password hint because, after suggesting one to Darlene, she said, "I don't think you can use swear words."

"Have you helped other people who've had these problems?" I asked.

"All the time," said Darlene.

"Has it ever happened to you?" I asked.

"Not at this company," Darlene replied. "But it's happened with other institutions."

"At this rate, I'll end up in an institution," I said. "The only way out is if I forget my password."

"The Buzz on Beeps"

If left to my own devices — the phone, the computer, the washing machine, the dryer, the dishwasher, the house alarm, the microwave, the doorbell camera, and even Alexa, the digital voice assistant — I would run them all over with my car because they won't stop beeping.

But then the car would start beeping and I would have to abandon the idea of silencing my inanimate tormenters and simply surrender to their incessant electronic nagging.

That's what I did when my cellphone erupted in a brief burst of beeping during the recent test of the Emergency Alert System.

Like millions of other Americans, I was warned about the test and worried it would be so maddening that I would be unable to call for help because, of course, the phone was beeping.

That it wasn't so bad meant I have accepted the sad fact that I am being bombarded daily with beeps, buzzes, rings, dings, and other annoying noises.

Not a moment goes by that some device or appliance doesn't go off.

The phone is worst offender. I am now convinced that Alexander Graham Bell should have been arrested for disturbing the peace and incarcerated in a cell with, yes, a cellphone that beeped and dinged so much that he had to call his assistant, Thomas Watson, and cry, "Watson, come here, I want you to make it stop!"

To which Watson would reply, "Text me."

And then hang up.

Bell would be both amazed and distressed by the fact that his invention is seldom used for talking anymore. If you want to call someone, you have to send a text, which entails typing a message. This happens so often that humans will soon be extinct because our opposable thumbs, the reason for our advanced development, will fall off.

At least we will no longer be subjected to our phones dinging with texts or beeping with irritating ringtones.

For now, however, we have to endure the seemingly endless auditory intrusions. And putting the phone on "silent mode" does little to alleviate the problem because you can still hear it vibrate, which makes the whole thing a mute point.

But the phone isn't the only guilty party. Our washing machine plays a little jingle when the laundry is done. Here it is: "Doo-doo, doo-doo-doo-doo-doo, doo-doo-doo, doo-doo-dooooo!"

And that's just the first part. After the second part, there is a pause, followed by the grand finale: "DOO-DOO-DOO!"

Not to be outdone, the dryer regales us with an electronic song I call "Dryer Beware," because it goes off when I am watching TV and am tempted to stomp into the laundry room and kick the stupid thing to death.

The dishwasher is no better. It beeps when you turn it on and plays its own song when the dishes are done. It also beeps if you accidentally lean against it. This happens even when it's not running.

Then there is the car. It beeps until I have put on my seatbelt. It beeps when I back up. It beeps when something — a car, a bird, a falling leaf — is approaching. It beeps when my left front tire goes exactly one millimeter onto a road stripe while I am changing lanes. It beeps when I turn off the car. And it beeps when I lock the vehicle. If I don't, it will beep. Then it will beep again when I get back in the car and start the whole routine over again.

I would drive the car off a cliff, but: (a) there are no cliffs where I live and (b) I would be in it.

Other machines and gadgets have added to the relentless assault. The only answer is to set fire to the house and destroy them all. With my luck, the smoke alarm will be the only device that doesn't work.

CHAPTER 7:

"WHAT'S UP, DOCS?"

"The Big Stuff Theory"

I've always considered myself top drawer, but the sad fact is that I'm bottom drawer, too. And it's all because my drawers are stuffed with drawers.

Every drawer in my house, as well as every closet, cabinet, and bin, is stuffed with stuff. It doesn't take a rocket scientist to understand that this is a problem. But it did take a rocket scientist to explain why.

"It's the law of physics," said my son-in-law Guillaume, an accelerator physicist who may not work with rockets but is a dedicated man of science and a great guy who works on a particle collider. He is destined, I proudly predict, to win the Nobel Prize.

I, on the other hand, am a lazy man of journalism who flunked science in school and thinks a collider is a car that has been in a fender bender. And if the vehicle happened to be mine, the particles would include protons, neutrons, and, of course, a moron. For that, I would no doubt win the Ig Nobel Prize.

Still, I reacted with the speed of light beer when I learned that physics is the reason my underwear can't fit in my dresser.

"No matter how many drawers you add to your bedroom, eventually all of them will be filled," Guillaume explained. "In physics, there is a theory that states that every empty space will eventually get filled. Everything has to be stable, everything radiates energy."

"Even my boxer shorts?" I asked.

"Basically, yes," Guillaume replied.

"I'm not stable," I said. "And I seldom radiate energy."

"You are a scientific wonder," said Guillaume, adding: "A French chemist named Antoine Lavoisier said, 'Nothing is lost, nothing is created, everything is transformed.' "

"And it's transformed in my house," I said.

"But there is a reverse corollary," Guillaume noted. "If you put something down in a specific place, something you know you need, like your car keys, and you tell yourself, 'Now I know where it is,' you won't be able to find it again."

I understood perfectly because Sue can never find any of the half-dozen or so pairs of eyeglasses she has scattered around the house.

"If I won Powerball, I'd never collect the money," I told Guillaume. "That's because Sue, a neat person, would inadvertently throw out the ticket or I, a messy person, would put it somewhere in the house and never find it."

"Don't worry," said Guillaume. "It's the same in my house. Spaces get filled and things we need can never be found."

I was beginning to comprehend this phenomenon because I could barely open my dresser drawers, one of which is jammed with underwear, another with socks, a third with T-shirts, and a fourth with pajamas.

In my office, there is a plastic bin with three drawers that are stuffed with sweatpants and sweatshirts. I have to sweat just to get them open.

The hall closet is filled with coats and jackets, as is the family room closet. The vast majority of the outerwear, I hasten to add, isn't mine. It belongs to Sue, who thoughtfully buys me the clothes that can't fit into my dresser drawers or in my bedroom closet, which is bulging with shirts, pants, suits, ties, and sport jackets, some of which I haven't worn in years.

The hall dresser has enough gloves, scarves, and knit caps to keep the entire population of Sweden warm.

Then there's the kitchen, which has one small holder containing approximately three dozen pens and pencils and a larger holder with spatulas, ladles, tongs, and other items that practically have to be hammered in. I'm surprised there isn't a hammer in there.

And there are the kitchen drawers, two of which have enough utensils for a state dinner and another that is filled to overflowing with pot holders, oven mitts, trivets, and so much other stuff that it couldn't be closed by a charging rhinoceros.

I don't even want to talk about the cabinets, though I will say that half of the world's coffee and tea could be poured into all the mugs we have.

The garage is also littered with stuff, but Sue recently came up with the great idea to transfer some of it to a space that has gone to waste since we moved in a quarter of a century ago: the attic.

The other day I lugged several boxes of Christmas stuff up there. Also moved to the attic was a large suitcase belonging to Lauren, who not only has been out of the house since the administration of George W. Bush but happens to be Guillaume's wife.

"Pretty soon, the attic will be filled, too," Guillaume predicted.

"And the only empty space in the house will be the one between my ears," I said observed.

"That's because you have too thick of a skull for anything to penetrate," Guillaume

"You're brilliant," I said. "If you don't win the Nobel Prize, the judges can go stuff it."

"Our Potholes Are Out of This World"

Space — the one between my ears — is the final frontier. Or

at least I thought so before I took a voyage in the car ship Zezima. My mission: to see an eminent astronomer and find out why lunar craters, Martian chasms, and other galactic bumps in the road are nothing compared to the potholes on my street.

"It's like driving on the surface of the moon," I told Fred Walter, a professor of astronomy at Stony Brook University on Long Island, New York. "I'm afraid I'll hit a pothole and go into a black hole."

"There's a hole on Mars called Pavonis Mons that's thirty-five meters across and twenty meters deep," said Prof. Walter, calculating that the measurements equal one hundred and fifteen feet by sixty-five feet. "That'll stall your car."

"That's nothing. There are some on the expressway that must be even bigger," I said. "I hit one the other day and thought my car would explode. Now I know how the astronauts felt when they drove those lunar rovers."

Prof. Walter knew I was referring to the vehicles used in the Apollo 15, 16, and 17 moon landings of 1971 and '72.

"They're like convertibles — no roofs," he said. "And no doors."

"The astronauts were lucky they didn't get thrown out when they hit a crater," I said. "I hope they were wearing seatbelts."

"Rovers don't have them," Prof. Walter said.

"At least there were no cops on the moon to give them a ticket," I noted.

Even though some lunar craters are comparable to terrestrial potholes, the astronauts never had to worry about blowing out a tire.

"The edges of moon craters tend to erode, so they're not as jagged as the potholes here on Earth," Prof. Walter said. "And rovers have metal mesh wheels, so they are a lot stronger than the tires on your car."

"I guess the astronauts didn't have to call AAA," I said, referring to what should be named the Aeronautical Assistance Association.

I told Prof. Walter that I took astronomy in college because I thought it would be fun.

"How did you do?" he asked.

"I almost flunked," I replied. "I didn't realize — because I was a stupid college student — that it involved math."

"I do as little math as possible," said Prof. Walter, who's sixty-seven and graduated from MIT in 1976.

"I knew all the planets," I said. "And I once saw a meteor shower. I figured that was enough."

"Astronomy is an observational science," Prof. Walter said, "but it's a lot more than just knowing the planets."

"Speaking of which," I said, "I was devastated when Pluto was demoted."

"It deserved to be," he said about the decision in 2006 by the International Astronomical Union to downgrade Pluto to the status of "dwarf planet."

"I bet the Disney Company had something to do with it," I said. "They probably thought the planet was competing with their cartoon dog."

"Nonsense," Prof. Walter said. "Pluto is tiny and far out. What would you rather be, the runt of the planets or the king of the dwarf planets?"

"I'm not even a star here on Earth," I said.

Another planetary controversy, I posited, is the correct pronunciation of "Uranus."

"It's not how you think it's pronounced," Prof. Walter said, a disappointing revelation for a jokester like yours truly. "But you can say it the funny way, too."

"Good," I said. "It's appropriate for a planet that's made of gas."

Uranus and the other gas giants — Jupiter, Saturn, and Neptune — don't have potholes because their surfaces aren't solid.

"But Pluto has them, right?" I asked Prof. Walter.

"In a manner of speaking," he said, explaining that the little rocky ball is covered in ice. "The surface has craters. If you want to call them potholes, go right ahead."

In addition to Earth and Mars, two other terrestrial planets — Mercury and Venus — have craters.

So, of course, does the moon.

"Some are very big and some are very small," said Prof. Walter, who has been teaching astronomy at Stony Brook for thirty-three years and is a fan of the original "Star Trek" TV series.

"I use a flip phone and it's usually turned off," he said. "I miss my old phone, which was the size and shape of a 'Star Trek' phaser. I could flip it open with one hand."

He also drives a 2007 Honda Civic.

"It has a stick shift," said Prof. Walter, who is married with two grown daughters and three grandchildren. "I taught one of my daughters to drive a stick shift when she was in high school. She said it impressed the boys."

"Have you hit any potholes?" I asked.

"Yes," he admitted. "There's one on Sheep Pasture Road that's huge. I hit it recently, but the car wasn't damaged. It's really well-built."

It helps, Prof. Walter said, to drive slowly.

"I go only five miles per hour over the speed limit," he said. "Maybe ten. I try to go around them."

He added that asteroid and meteor strikes and the freeze-thaw cycle contribute to the creation of craters and, of course, potholes.

"The universe surprises us," Prof. Walter told me. "It's always expanding. Everything gets emptier with time."

"My head has already achieved that," I said.

"No comment," the good professor replied.

"Admit it," I said. "The space between my ears would make for a pretty good pothole."

"These Folks Are Good Medicine"

I have never been an ambulance chaser, mainly because I can't run that fast, but if the producers of "Chicago Fire" are looking for a stunt driver, or even a guest star to provide comic relief, I'd be happy to sign up.

In a scene straight out of the popular TV show, I jumped in my car and managed to keep up with an emergency vehicle that rushed Sue to the hospital, where she was successfully treated for an intestinal issue and I should have been admitted for having a bleeding knuckle and only half a brain.

The adventure began a little after midnight, when Sue complained of the same symptoms she had when she suffered a heart attack late last year.

Springing into action, which almost resulted in a sprained ankle, I called 911.

About five minutes later, an ambulance pulled into the driveway and a pair of paramedics, Tom and Steve, knocked on the door.

"You're bleeding." Tom said when I let them in.

I looked at the knuckle on the middle finger of my right hand

and said, "I have dry skin."

"You called an ambulance for that?" Steve said incredulously.

"No, but if you have a Band-Aid, I'd appreciate it," I replied. "Actually, it's my wife. I think she's having a heart attack."

I led the dynamic duo into the family room, where Sue was sitting in a chair. They gave her an EKG (results: normal) and gave me a warning.

"Don't try to follow us," Tom said.

"People do that all the time," Steve added. "They run red lights and stop signs to keep up with us."

After Sue was put into the back of the ambulance, Tom said to me, "We'll see you at the hospital. Drive safely!"

Sue said later that the guys regaled her with stories during the ride.

"Crazy drivers are constantly bumping the ambulance," Tom told her. "I can't tell you the number of times I've been knocked around."

"One time I hit my noggin on the door," Steve chimed in.

"This is fun!" Sue squealed. "It's like 'Chicago Fire.' "

Tom shook his head and responded, "We're better than 'Chicago Fire.' "

Ten minutes later, I met Sue and the paramedics at the hospital.

"Some idiot was right on our tail," Sue said while lying on a stretcher in the emergency room.

"It was me," I confessed.

"We tell people not to do that," Tom said. "The one person we don't tell is the one who will do that."

"If I got pulled over by a cop, I would have said you told me it was OK," I said.

"Thanks for having our backs," said Steve.

"You guys are the ones who should be thanked," I told the two paramedics. "You're lifesavers."

"Wintergreen?" Tom asked.

"Yes," I answered. "The best kind."

Overhearing this exchange, Sue confided, "It's a good thing I brushed my teeth."

"Otherwise, I could just imagine the diagnosis," I told her. "Bad breath."

After Tom and Steve left, a nurse took Sue's vitals. Then I gave her a list of the medications that Sue has to take.

"I never used to take anything," Sue said. "Now I have my own pharmacy."

When Sue was settled in Chest Pain One, a unit next to the ER, a doctor came in and said, "Susan?"

"No," I replied. "I'm Jerry. This," I added, pointing to the patient, "is Susan."

As the doctor examined Sue, a woman from the billing department, who was on the job at one a.m., handed me a piece of paper. It was headlined "Your Rights and Protections Against Surprise Medical Bills."

"I don't like bills, even if they're not a surprise," I told her.

"I don't blame you," she said.

"Can I make this into a paper airplane and fly it across the room?" I asked.

"Sure," she replied. "I just gave a copy to the patient on the other side. You can fly the planes to each other."

Unfortunately, there wasn't time for an air show because the nurse had to take Sue's blood. She tends to pass out when this happens, so I had to hold her hand — the other one was where the needle would go — and assure her that it would be all right. This entailed telling her stupid jokes to distract her.

"Don't worry," I said. "It won't be in vain. Well, actually, it will be in vein, but it won't be in vain."

The nurse chuckled. Sue rolled her eyes.

"I think I'm going to pass out," I said, feigning a faint.

Sue smiled and said, "Stop it!"

I stopped at three-thirty a.m., when it was decided that Sue would stay and I would go.

When I returned the following afternoon, I greeted Sue, who had slept comfortably, and went to the nurses' station because my knuckle was bleeding again.

"Would you by any chance have a Band-Aid?" I asked.

"A Band-Aid? What's that?" said a nurse named Victoria.

"I just found the last one," said Kristen, a nurse's assistant.

When she gave me a plain adhesive bandage, I said, "Thanks, but don't you have Hello Kitty or Care Bears Band-Aids?"

"Not even Smurfs," Kristen said.

"We're getting Batman next week," Victoria added.

In the next bed, on the other side of the curtain, was Jim, a heart patient who was being visited by his wife, Bonnie.

"I have plaque," Jim told me.

"You should see a dentist," I replied.

"I already blew off a dental appointment the other day," Jim said. "Now I have plaque in my heart, too."

A hospital staffer named Don came in to give Sue a nuclear stress test.

He prepped her with saline, then said, "Here's the chaser."

"How about red wine?" I suggested. "It's good for the heart."

"We serve that at dinner," said Don, adding that the test tricks the body into thinking it's getting exercise.

"When I watch sports on TV, do I trick my body into thinking it's getting exercise?" I asked.

"Sure, if your body really thinks so," Don replied.

"Since this test is nuclear, will Sue be radioactive?" I wondered.

"No," said Don, "but you could cut down on your electric bill."

I looked at Sue and said, "You glow, girl!"

All the tests administered to Sue, including a CT scan, showed that she wasn't having heart issues.

"My colon is swollen," she informed me.

"Hey," I said, "that rhymes!"

It wasn't pleasant, but the news was good because things could have been worse. The three stents that were inserted when Sue had her heart attack a little over three months ago were working fine.

"I guess they're still under warranty," I noted.

Sue, who hadn't eaten in twenty-four hours, wolfed down a meal of chicken, rice, and carrots before she was released.

Full credit goes to the doctors, nurses, and technicians at John T. Mather Memorial Hospital, as well as to the paramedics at the Coram Fire Department, for taking such good care of Sue.

"Thanks for saving my life," I said to the nurses as we were leaving.

"That's our job," replied Victoria.

Kristen smiled and added, "You owe us a Band-Aid."

"The Sound of Joking"

I am not above stealing from William Shakespeare, whose relatives can't take me to court because he wanted to kill all the lawyers, which is why I implore friends, Romans, countrymen, and anybody who is not on the phone: Lend me your ears.

I make this urgent plea because Sue thinks I can't hear. I say the same about her. It has, unfortunately, fallen on deaf ears.

So I went to an ear, nose, and throat specialist to have the potatoes removed from my auditory canal and to find out if spouses have failure to communicate because they really ought to be in a hearing-aid commercial.

I raised the subject with Sue — and had to repeat myself — after the following conversation.

Sue: (Inaudible)

Me: "What?"

Sue: "I was talking to myself."

Later, we had this exchange.

Sue: (Inaudible)

Me: (No response)

Sue: "You don't listen to a word I say."

Me: "I thought you were talking to yourself."

Sue: "I was talking to you."

Me: "What?"

I don't talk to myself even though no one else, principally Sue, wants to hear what I have to say. And when we are watching

TV and she has the remote, I frequently have to ask her to jack up the volume to a decibel level that is high enough to blow out the windows.

"You need the wax taken out of your ears," said Sue, who suggested I go to the medical group where she had her own earwax removed.

A week later, as I sat in the office of otolaryngology, which I can't pronounce and couldn't spell without looking it up, nurse practitioner ToniAnn Savage said, "Sometimes I feel like a therapist for couples who can't hear each other."

"My wife's hearing seems much better since you took the wax out of her ears," I said. "Her only complaint is that she can now hear all of my stupid jokes."

When ToniAnn pointed a light into my left ear, I asked, "Can you see all the way to the other side?"

"Very clearly," she said with a smile.

Then she began to remove wax from both of my ears.

"You could cut the time in half if I were Vincent van Gogh," I told her.

ToniAnn sighed and said, "I think your wife is just ignoring you."

"It looks like I have quite a potato crop," I said when ToniAnn showed me what she had removed.

"It's not that bad," she said. "By the way, did you recently get a haircut?"

"Last week," I answered. "Why?"

"Because," said ToniAnn, "you have two hairs in your left ear. The next time you get a haircut, you should ask the barber to put cotton in your ears."

"Then I really won't be able to hear," I said.

After ToniAnn had finished, she introduced me to Deena Palumbo, a doctor of audiology, who would be giving me a hearing test.

"My wife passed the test and says she can now hear all of my stupid jokes," I said.

"Are you getting a divorce?" Deena asked.

"No," I replied. "I wouldn't hear of it."

For my test, I sat in a soundproof booth and put on a pair of earphones, through which Deena, who was just outside, sent a series of words and beeps at different decibels. I had to tell her what I was hearing.

"You scored very well," Deena said afterward. "You can definitely hear your wife, but if you don't want to tell her the test results, it will be our secret."

"How is your hearing?" I asked.

"Pristine," Deena said proudly. "I can hear everything my husband and kids say. But if I diagnose a patient with hearing loss, the advice I give is to call the spouse's name before you say something. If you have to say, 'What?' three times, it's like baseball: You've struck out."

When I got home, Sue asked, "How did you do?"

I cupped my hand to my ear and said, "What?"

"Just What the Doctors Ordered"

Laughter, goes an old saying, is the best medicine. And, I would add, because I'm old myself, the cheapest.

It was the prescription for a smooth transition from my old doctor, who always told me jokes but is now retiring, to my new physician, who not only has an excellent sense of humor but is the only doctor I have ever had who is younger than I am.

My former medicine man, Dr. Antoun Mitromaras, is hanging up his stethoscope after more than half a century of doctoring.

"What are you going to do in retirement?" I asked him during my last office visit.

"Watch TV," said Dr. Mitromaras, who is eighty-one.

He's the guy who gave me the best medical advice ever. I once asked him if he had seen those commercials for prescription medications with side effects that include death.

"Yes," Dr. Mitromaras said.

"Have patients asked you about them?" I wanted to know.

"Yes," the good doctor replied.

"What do you tell them?" I wondered.

"If they can kill you," he said, "don't take them."

He also told me jokes that were often too risqué to repeat here.

"Tell me one I can repeat in polite company," I said.

"This guy dies and goes to the Pearly Gates," Dr. Mitromaras began. "St. Peter says, 'I'll let you in if you can relieve me for a little while. I'm tired and want to take a nap.' The guy asks what he has to do. St. Peter says, 'Ask anyone who shows up how to spell love. If they get it right, let them in. If not, send them downstairs.' Several people show up and spell love correctly, so the guy lets them in. Then his mother-in-law arrives. The guy has never gotten along with her. She says, 'I hear there's a spelling test' The guy nods and says, 'Spell Czechoslovakia.' "

I didn't expect to have as many laughs with my new physician, Dr. Sanjay Sangwan, but I had a great time during my initial visit.

"You have a pulse," he informed me. "And a heartbeat."

"That's good to know," I said. "Do I have brain activity?"

"I'd have to run some tests to make sure," replied Dr. Sangwan, who just turned fifty-one.

"You're the first doctor I have ever had who is younger than I am," I told him.

"How old are you?" he inquired.

"I'm a little more than a year away from being seventy," I said.

Dr. Sangwan raised his eyebrows in surprise and said, "You look like you're in your fifties."

"God bless you," I said, shaking his hand. "By the way, how's your eyesight?"

"You got me there," he said, adjusting his glasses. "But I see by your family history that longevity is common."

"Yes," I said. "My mother is about to turn ninety-eight. And she's sharper than I am. Of course, so are houseplants, but that's another story."

"You have good genes," Dr. Sangwan told me.

"My wife bought my jeans," I said, pointing to my denim pants. "I have more at home."

The doctor looked over my paperwork and said, "You've had kidney stones."

"Six or seven," I noted. "I regret to say that I've had to number them like the Super Bowl."

"They can be painful," Dr. Sangwan said.

"When I had my first one, a nurse told me that it's the male equivalent of childbirth," I said. "I told her that at least I wouldn't have to put the stone through college."

When I mentioned I have another one that is tucked away on

my right side, Dr. Sangwan said, "Keep an eye on it."

"I can't lower my head that far," I said.

He smiled and said, "You've really brightened my morning."

Dr. Sangwan and his wonderful staff brightened mine, too.

"Welcome to the practice," he said as I headed out.

"It's nice to be your newest patient even though I'm really old," I said. "And that's no joke."

"Going Viral"

The great humorist Erma Bombeck said that no one ever died from sleeping in an unmade bed.

I'm glad Erma was right because otherwise Sue and I would now be in the Great Bed, Bath & Beyond.

We spent the better part of a week in the sack while being sacked by COVID-19. Just when we thought it was safe to go out — after three years of being masked, tasked, and vaxxed to the max — we somehow contracted the virus. And we think we got it from, of all people, Lady Liberty.

Sue and I — with Lauren, Katie, Dave, and all five grandchildren — went to the Statue of Liberty but couldn't get in because the tickets were sold out.

It was just as well because climbing those three hundred and fifty-four stairs probably would have induced cardiac arrest. Then I'd really be bedridden. I can't even make it up the twelve stairs in my house without getting winded.

But the long cool woman in a green dress wasn't wearing a mask. Neither were we and the hundreds of people we encountered on Liberty Island.

Sue and I were among the huddled masses yearning to breathe free. A couple of days later, we had trouble breathing, which is nothing to sneeze at.

We sneezed anyway. We also coughed, ached, and drank so much water — because we were told to keep well-hydrated — that our pet fish was getting nervous.

The bathroom was like Grand Central Station. I was tempted to hang a sign over the toilet: "All aboard!"

Yes, these were flush times in our house.

But back to bed, where we spent so much time — one night I slept for eleven hours and Sue for twelve — that it could have been considered hibernation.

Sometimes one of us went back to bed for a nap shortly after getting up in the morning while the other took the afternoon shift. Most days Sue also napped on the couch. One day I took two naps. Another day we napped in bed together but faced away from each other because we didn't want to catch what we already had.

Now you know why neither of us went to med school.

Speaking of which, our doctors were sympathetic but essentially powerless to do anything to help us except, in my case, prescribe Paxlovid, an antiviral medication, and, in both cases, tell us to drink enough liquids to drown a walrus.

And, of course, get plenty of rest.

Day after agonizing day, the bed remained unmade. There was no point in making it because: (a) at least one of us would only go back to it and (b) we weren't expecting a visit from Good Housekeeping.

Somehow, we remained alive.

It was a miracle considering I ran a fever high enough to fry an egg on my head, dummy side up.

Sue ran hot and cold — a fever, then chills — but had it worse than I did because she's a heart patient and couldn't take any medicine stronger than Tylenol.

So we napped. We hadn't napped this much since we were babies. At one point, I felt like crying for a bottle, but my doctor said I couldn't have beer. It was horrible.

Being in a high-risk category — old — didn't help.

Still, it made us wonder: How did this happen? We thought the pandemic was over. We had taken all precautions and had escaped the virus. Until now.

Sue said even her heart attack two years ago wasn't as bad as this. Neither of us had ever been sicker.

But we survived. Tragically, millions of other people didn't.

A few family members and friends have also had the coronavirus. Some cases were mild, some serious, including one case of long COVID.

Fortunately, Sue and I are feeling much better.

Good Housekeeping can come over now. The bed has finally been made.

"Off-the-Cuff Remarks"

If you need a shoulder to cry on, don't blubber all over mine. I'm crying on my own shoulder these days because I have an injured rotator cuff.

This means, unfortunately, that I won't be able to pitch in the major leagues or make game-winning shots in the NBA.

My mother once tore her rotator cuff in a fall down the stairs and couldn't play in our family Wiffle ball league, where she was an ace hurler who set a record for strikeouts, mostly against me.

And my rotator-cuff issue will prevent me from taking on LeBron James because I can't even make three-pointers when I try to shoot napkin balls into the garbage can in the kitchen.

"You missed," Sue often huffs as she picks them up.

"No, I didn't," I respond feebly. "I was aiming for the floor."

But it's no use. My sports career, which was just getting started even though I am almost seventy years old, is over.

That's what my doctor suggested when I went for a routine examination and complained about the pain in my right shoulder.

"It's your rotator cuff," he said after asking me to raise my sore arm above my empty head. "I don't know if it's torn, but I suspect it's calcified."

"I thought the only thing in my body that's calcified is my brain," I said.

"That would be a bigger problem," the doctor said. "But you need to go for physical therapy."

I made an appointment at a rehabilitation center and saw Danielle Bifolco, an excellent and personable physical therapist who asked how I injured my rotator cuff.

"Either bench-pressing my grandchildren or doing twelve-ounce curls," I replied.

Danielle asked me to sit in a chair and look directly at her.

"Your posture could be better," she informed me. "You're a little off."

"I've been off for years," I confessed.

"You're tilted a bit," she said.

"Like the Leaning Tower of Pisa?" I wondered.

"And you're stiff," Danielle added as she checked out my upper torso.

"This is more serious than I thought," I said. "I hope rigor mortis isn't setting in."

"I don't think so," said Danielle, who asked me to turn my head.

I winced and said, "I'm a pain in my own neck."

"Lift your left arm," Danielle instructed.

"It feels OK," I said.

"Now lift your right arm," she said.

"Ouch!" I shrieked.

"Are you right-handed?" Danielle asked.

"I'm ambidextrous," I told her. "Incompetent with both hands."

After putting me through more routines — pushing out, up and down against her hands, reaching down to touch my upper spine with each hand, and reaching up with each hand to touch the middle of my back, all of which sent lightning bolts through my right shoulder — Danielle said, "I think your infraspinatus muscle is irritated."

She explained that the infraspinatus is one of the four muscles of the rotator cuff.

"Its function is to rotate the humerus," Danielle said.

"There's nothing humorous about it," I replied.

"I am going to put you on a home exercise program," she said.

The first exercise entailed standing in a doorway and, using a folded towel as a cushion, pushing my right arm against the frame.

"You've got me in a jamb," I noted.

Danielle smiled and said, "You could do it against a wall, too."

"I'm off the wall," I told her. "Will it still work?"

"With you, I don't know," said Danielle, who gave me a printout of the exercises, which included the isometric internal rotation, isometric external rotation, and isometric abduction. Each set should be done for ten seconds and repeated ten times. The exercises should be performed four times a week.

"They will help strengthen your rotator cuff," Danielle said. "Just be careful when you bench-press your grandchildren. And enjoy the twelve-ounce curls."

CHAPTER 8:
"MISCELLANEOUS MUSINGS"

"Hooked on Crocheting"

Ever since I could talk, which led to the invention of earplugs, I have been pulling the wool over everyone's eyes by spinning yarns. Now I am using the wool in a ball of yarn to make a blanket that you can pull over your eyes and, since I can't stop talking about it, your ears, too.

That's because I have taken up crocheting.

I got hooked when I saw Sue making a blanket for one of our young grandchildren. So I needled her to show me how it's done.

First, I had to learn the basics.

"Are we working with yarn or wool?" I asked.

"Yarn," Sue answered.

"What's yarn made of?" I wanted to know.

"Wool," said Sue.

I sighed and asked if she was using a hook or a needle.

"A hook," Sue said. "Now," she added, handing it to me, "take this needle."

"I thought it was called a hook," I said.

"It is," Sue replied.

"This is going to be complicated," I said.

Sue shook her head and said, "I might need a glass of wine."

Thus began my first crochet tutorial, in which I proved to be a knit wit.

The main problem was digital.

"You have sausage fingers," Sue told me.

"Hot or mild?" I asked.

"Neither," she responded. "They're too fat."

In other words, I was all thumbs. It explained why I had an almost impossible time with the simplest stuff, like getting looped, which did not involve the wine Sue said she might need.

"Hold the hook in your right hand, the wool in your left, and cross over to make a loop," she instructed.

When I couldn't get the hang of it, Sue said, "Follow my hands." Then she showed me how to pull the wool through the loop.

"Make a circle through the first hole," she said. "Take the yarn, wrap it around, and pull it through."

Then she said we were going to make something called a Chain 3.

"So far," I noted, "it's Chain 3, Jerry 0."

Sue shook her head again.

"I can see I don't have you in stitches," I said.

"You don't have the yarn in stitches, either," she retorted.

"Let me try again," I said.

I fumbled the yarn, which kept falling off my index finger. I was going to use the middle finger, but Sue said it wouldn't be proper crochet etiquette.

Time after time I tried to make stitches, loops, circles, chains, and double crochets, also known as DCs. My efforts weren't successful because I am another DC: dumb crocheter. Finally, with Sue's expert guidance and eternal patience, I managed to pull the wool through two loops, then two more.

"You did it!" Sue squealed. "Hooray!"

It was just the initial step in making a six-inch square, thirty of which would be needed to complete the blanket.

Sue had to make dinner, so she suggested I go on YouTube and watch a video tutorial called "Hooked by Robin."

In it, a nice Englishwoman named Batman (no, I mean Robin) used her fingers to walk me through the process of making what is known in crochet circles as a granny square.

"I'm going back to basics with the humble granny square," Robin said at the beginning of the half-hour video. "This tutorial is for total beginners. So grab a cup of tea and crochet your very first granny square with me."

I made myself a cup of Earl Grey, naturally, and went back to the video, which featured Robin's slender fingers, a hook, and some yarn.

"I'm going to show you how to do the first three rounds," Robin said. "Then I'm going to show you how to change color."

I wondered if the audience included chameleons.

Robin did what Sue showed me how to do, except I couldn't stop her to ask questions or make stupid jokes. So I had to go back and rewatch certain parts.

Eventually, I got the hang of it and actually replicated my triumph with Sue.

I stopped the video and ran to show her.

"You did OK," Sue said approvingly. "Your stitches are tight, but you're doing a good job. You just have to practice. After a while, it becomes second nature."

"With me," I said, "it's more like ninety-second nature."

"That's not the half of it," Sue said. "Once you make all these squares, you have to sew them together. It's very time-consuming."

"I don't mind," I said. "I just want to make a blanket that the kids will enjoy."

"By the time you're   finished," Sue predicted, "they might be in college."

"I Need Moe Money"

If I had spent twenty-four thousand dollars on a wrought iron weathervane depicting the Three Stooges in their famous eye-poking stance, would my wife hit me over the head with an auctioneer's hammer?

Soitenly! Nyuk, nyuk, nyuk!

That's why, despite being a lifelong Stooges fan, I resisted the temptation to bid an amount higher than $4.85 on any of the dozens of items in the Moe Howard and Norman Maurer Estate Auction.

Moe, of course, was the Stooges' leader, the one with the sugar-bowl haircut who bragged that he was "the brains of the outfit." As a character in one of their short subjects pointed out, "It isn't saying very much." Maurer was Moe's real-life son-in-law.

And $4.85 was the amount the Stooges were left with, after taxes, when Curly won fifty thousand dollars in a radio contest in the 1938 classic "Healthy, Wealthy and Dumb."

So even if I had won fifty grand in the lottery, Sue, who like most women is not a fan of the legendary comedy trio, wouldn't let me bid on any of the Stooge-related merchandise in the online auction.

Still, I wanted to find out more about this slapstick treasure trove, so I called Nate D. Sanders Auctions, the Los Angeles company that conducted the sale, and spoke with consignment coordinator Jamie Perez.

"Are you a Three Stooges fan?" I wondered.

"I appreciate their genius," she responded.

"Most women hate the Stooges," I said admiringly. "You are in a select group. Who's your favorite Stooge?"

"I'd have to say Curly," Jamie said. "Who's yours?"

"Shemp," I answered. "The surest sign of maturity in a man, if indeed it ever happens, is when he comes to appreciate Shemp."

"I like that," said Jamie, adding that at the auction house, she wears "many hats."

"Is one of them a derby?" I asked. "It's what Curly wore."

"No," said Jamie, who asked if I wanted to bid on any items, which included Curly's eighteen-karat gold ring and Moe's ketubah, the Jewish marriage contract for his 1925 wedding to his wife, Helen.

"I'm limiting myself to $4.85," I said.

"You'll have to start higher than that," Jamie informed me. "Do you have Venmo?"

"I don't have Venmoe, Venlarry, or Vencurly," I responded, "although I'm trying to get Venshemp."

"You could be a Stooge, too," Jamie said.

I responded to this supreme compliment by saying, "Thanks, toots!"

I was also grateful that she put me in touch with Sam Heller, of Sam Heller Communications, which represents several auction houses, including Nate D. Sanders Auctions.

"Did you know that Shemp's real name was Sam?" I asked him.

"I had no idea," said Sam.

"And Curly's real name was Jerry," I added.

"You are an encyclopedia of Three Stooges trivia," Sam said.

He was even more impressed when I told him that this is the

hundredth anniversary of the team, which was founded in 1922 when a vaudeville headliner named Ted Healy enlisted Moe Howard and his older brother Shemp as his first sidekicks, or "stooges." Larry Fine joined the act three years later.

"The centennial is even more reason for collectors to own memorabilia from one of the greatest comedy teams of all time," said Sam.

"Who's your favorite Stooge?" I asked.

"That's like asking who your favorite child is," Sam answered. "But I'd have to say Larry."

"Did you know," I said, "that the Stooges were nominated for an Academy Award for Best Short Subject of 1934 for 'Men in Black'?"

"It's much better than the 'Men in Black' with Will Smith," Sam opined.

"And Moe delivered better slaps than Will," I said.

Sam heartily agreed.

The auction concluded the next day, with the weathervane going for $24,079, Moe's marriage contract for $21,889, and Curly's ring for $10,456.

When I told Sue about it, she said, "If you had spent that kind of money, I would have brained you."

"It wouldn't take much," I replied. "Woo woo woo!"

"Raised Seal of Approval"

I have driven every boat I have ever been on, including a cruise ship that miraculously did not, with me at the helm, end up in Davy Jones's locker.

My sole qualification for being a captain who could put the "Love Boat" skipper to shame: I had a New York State driver's license.

Now I can pilot a vessel to Mexico or Canada, or just be a passenger with both hands on deck after becoming seasick, because I recently got an enhanced license.

The license is for driving a car (I don't need one to drive people crazy), but it has honors and benefits beyond those of the standard driver's license, chief of which is the legal ability to flee the country in case the Feds are after me. And, let's face it, this is inevitable.

Several weeks ago, I went to the DMV — which in my case stands for the Department of Multiple Violations, none of which I have been ticketed for — to get an enhanced license.

I needed several items to prove that I am, indeed, myself; that I was, in fact, born and not created by a mad scientist ("It's alive! It's alive!"); and that I live in my home, sweet home.

This entailed providing my Social Security card, a bill from the electric company with my residential address on it, and — here's where it got troublesome — my birth certificate.

Unfortunately, my copy of the latter document didn't have a raised seal.

A sympathetic person at the DMV said I needed the genuine article or I couldn't get an enhanced driver's license.

So on a recent trip to my hometown of Stamford, Connecticut, I stopped off at the city and town clerk's office in the Government Center to get an original version of my birth certificate.

I was helped by a very nice and efficient assistant registrar named Diane, who asked when I was born.

"It was so long ago that my birth certificate is probably on a stone tablet," I replied.

This did not deter Diane, who returned exactly seven minutes later with a copy, on paper, of my birth certificate.

"Does it have a raised seal?" I asked.

"Yes," answered Diane, who showed it to me.

"I thought I would have to go to an aquarium for a raised seal," I said.

Another personable assistant registrar named Karin asked why I needed my birth certificate.

"I want to get an enhanced driver's license," I replied. "I'll need it if I have to skip town."

"You're good to go," Karin said. "We won't tell anyone we saw you."

A couple of days later, I went back to the DMV, where I was helped, quickly and pleasantly, by Tara, who worked at Window 11.

"Do you have all your documents?" she asked.

"Here they are," I said, handing her my Social Security card and my electric bill.

"That's not bad," Tara said when she saw the bill. "I pay more than you do."

"I would have brought a bank statement," I said, "but there's not much in the account."

"I know the feeling," Tara said.

"And here," I said, "is my birth certificate. It even has a raised seal."

"That means you're you," Tara noted.

"Nobody else would want to be me," I said, adding that my enhanced driver's license would enable me to fly anywhere.

"Not really," Tara informed me. "You'll still need a passport. The enhanced license will allow you to fly within the United States. You can also drive to Canada or Mexico. Or you can take a boat."

"I have a boat," I said, "but it's in my bathtub."

"I guess you won't get very far," Tara said.

"Not unless I take a cruise to Mexico," I said. "And with my enhanced driver's license, I could be the captain."

"You Axed for It"

In my hands, which are big and clumsy, tools are dangerous weapons, which is why I generally avoid using saws, hammers, drills, and other menacing objects that could slice off a finger, crush a thumb, pummel a palm, or otherwise destroy my hands.

So imagine my surprise and delight to find out that — in my right hand, at least — I am a natural with an axe.

I don't mean using one to chop wood (not a good idea since I don't have a fireplace and the house might burn down), but rather throwing one at a target.

And I consistently hit the bull's-eye, which is no bull, by displaying a good eye at the New York Axe Throwing Range, where I didn't need beginner's luck to show that I am a champ at burying the hatchet.

My axe-ploits (more axe puns coming up!) impressed coach Liz Vanek and manager Kaitlyn Lombardi, who agreed that I have an inherent talent at an activity that was popular during the Middle Ages. I considered it good timing since I will be the big Seven-Oh on my next birthday and, unless I live to be a hundred and forty, am a bit past middle age.

"Am I the oldest axe thrower you've ever met?" I asked.

"No," said Liz. "We had a sweet little old lady in her eighties who was really good. She said, 'I've never thrown axes before.' But she wanted to try. And she killed it."

"Killed?" I stammered.

"Not literally," Liz assured me.

Before I tried my hand at throwing caution to the wind, I said to Liz and Kaitlyn, "Let's get the wordplay out of the way. Do you hear a lot of axe puns, like 'You axed for it' and 'It's a hatchet job'?"

"All the time," Liz quickly acknowledged. "The puns make me groan internally."

"We've even come up with our own," said Kaitlyn, who told me about the names of teams that customers could use.

They included VIP Axe-cess, Axe-cent, Axe-ident, My Axe Husband, My Axe Wife, and, the best one, Pain in the Axe.

"We already did the work for you," Kaitlyn noted.

"Thank you," I said. "I'm happy to axe-cept your help."

And I couldn't have been in better — or younger — hands.

Liz is eighteen and became a certified axe-throwing coach after going through a rigorous training program that involved learning safety measures, becoming proficient at consistently hitting the target, and — this is very important — not maiming anybody.

"No missing limbs," she said.

Kaitlyn is twenty-one and used to work as a clown at birthday parties.

"I'm a pretty good axe thrower," said Kaitlyn, who started in the entertainment industry. "But Liz is better. After all, she's a coach."

"Let's see how you do," Liz said as she brought me to the first of the range's fourteen lanes.

"Are you right-handed or left-handed?" she asked.

"I'm ambidextrous," I replied. "I'm incompetent with both hands."

"Some people use both to throw axes," Liz said. "But which hand is more dominant?"

"My right one," I answered.

"That's important to know because of leg placement," she said. "You have to put your best foot forward."

"Another pun!" I exclaimed.

"Sorry," Liz said softly.

But first, I had to choose one of two kinds of axes: a smaller one, which resembled a hatchet, and a larger one that was a genuine axe.

I chose the smaller one because, as I told Liz, "I don't have an axe to grind."

She groaned internally and handed it to me.

"Bring it back like this," she said, helping me hold the axe next to my head and parallel to the floor while standing a dozen feet from the large wooden target. "Step into your throw and follow through. The axe should rotate once before hitting the target. Ready?"

"Ready!" I said. Then I let the axe fly.

It landed squarely in the middle of the target.

"Bull's-eye!" Liz chirped as she rang a bell.

"Great shot!" added Kaitlyn.

I had several more throws, the majority of which were bull's-eyes.

Then I switched to the larger axe, for which I had to stand a couple of feet farther from the target. It didn't matter. I scored one bull's-eye after another.

This continued for an hour (the price for which is thirty-nine dollars). I could have gone for an hour and a half (fifty-five dollars), but I had already proved my point.

"You are very good at throwing axes," said Liz.

"Did you have fun?" asked Kaitlyn.

I smiled proudly and said, "I had an axe-cellent time."

"Those Are the Brakes"

At the risk of throwing myself under the bus, which isn't much of a risk because the bus is stopped, I plead guilty to passing a stopped school bus.

I couldn't believe I had done something so stupid — and I do stupid things all the time — because I don't text and drive, I stop at red lights and stop signs, and I obey the speed limit. Or at least I don't drive like a white-knuckled, lead-footed NASCAR wannabe.

I am especially careful in school zones and am always aware, no matter where I am, of school buses.

Except this time.

The proof came when I got a notice in the mail informing me of my transportation transgression.

On the citation was photographic evidence that I had violated New York Vehicle and Traffic Law Section 1174-a. There also was the link to a video, which I watched. Sure enough, I saw my car pass the red stop sign that extended from the side of the bus.

Amount due: two hundred and fifty dollars.

I had two choices: I could fight this all the way to the Supreme Court (as my own defense attorney, I'd probably end up in Sing Sing). Or I could admit guilt, promise to mend my ways, and pay the fine.

I chose the latter.

But first, I drove (very carefully) to the Suffolk County

Traffic and Parking Violations Agency to see what creative excuses people use when they go to traffic court.

In the ticket office, where I got number Q689, I spoke with a defense attorney named Lindsay, who remembered one rather offbeat defendant.

"This motorcyclist was going at an excessive rate of speed and wiped out," Lindsay recalled. "The judge said, 'Is it true you were doing a hundred and twenty-five miles an hour?' The guy said, 'No, Your Honor. I was only doing a hundred and ten.' He still had to pay a big fine, but at least he lived."

"Have you ever had a traffic violation?" I asked.

"Not that I'll admit," Lindsay replied.

In the conference room, where dozens of defendants waited to see a judge, I met Sean and Natasha, both representing themselves in their respective cases.

"I'm here because I was driving a commercial vehicle on a parkway," said Sean.

"Was it a big rig?" I asked.

"No, it was a van," answered Sean, who is twenty-three. "I also got a ticket for advertising. I work for a wholesale seafood company with its name, address, and phone number on the side of the vehicle."

"I'm sorry to say this," said Natasha, who sat next to Sean, "but that's stupid."

"It sounds fishy," I added.

Sean, who missed his previous court date because, he explained, "I forgot," said he hoped to get one of the charges dropped.

"It doesn't always work," he said. "My brother is a cop, so I have a police union card. One time I got stopped for speeding. I handed the cop the card along with my license. He threw the card back at me."

"At least he was honest," I noted.

"Unfortunately," Sean said.

Natasha was there because she backed into another car in the parking lot at work.

"What's your excuse?" I asked her.

"I'm a teenage girl," said Natasha, who's eighteen.

"I'm not a lawyer, but I don't think that will stand up in court," I said.

"Probably not," Natasha conceded. "The real reason is that it was the end of the day and I was in a hurry to get home."

Both she and Sean said they have received other citations in their brief driving careers but insisted that older drivers, like yours truly, are worse than young ones, like them.

"You drive too slow," said Natasha, who admitted that, like me, she had once been fined for driving past a stopped school bus.

"It cost me more than three hundred dollars," she remembered.

A few minutes later, Natasha's name was called. I wished Sean luck and accompanied her to a small courtroom, where she pleaded guilty and was fined two hundred and twenty dollars.

"Thank you, Your Honor," Natasha said before leaving.

"You're very welcome. Have a nice day," replied the Honorable Jeffrey Arlen Spinner, who is so nice that he would put Judge Judy to shame.

Judge Spinner, who practices law in New York and Connecticut, was wearing a necktie with pictures of cars on it.

"That's perfect for traffic court," I noted.

"I'm a motor head," the judge said.

"Have you ever gotten a driving citation?" I wondered.

"Of course," he answered. "Who hasn't?"

His last one was in 1989.

"I've been careful ever since," said Judge Spinner, a fellow father and grandfather who treats defendants with dignity and respect. "It's what every person who comes before me in court is entitled to," he said. "You never know what their stories are."

"My story is that I passed a stopped school bus," I admitted.

"It happens," Judge Spinner said. "Just make sure to pay the fine. And drive home safely."

"Getting Trivial With Alexa"

Here is today's trivia challenge: What modern figure was famously described by his wife as "an encyclopedia of useless information"?

(a) Albert Einstein

(b) Alex Trebek

(c) Pat Sajak

(d) Jerry Zezima

If you guessed (d), you are correct! Unfortunately, you do not win a Caribbean cruise or cash and prizes totaling one hundred thousand dollars, but you do have my eternal (or at least temporary) gratitude.

Sue, who used to think I didn't know anything worth knowing, now knows better.

That's because she and I teamed up to score our one thousandth point in Question of the Day, a game of knowledge hosted by Alexa, the virtual assistant who operates on artificial intelligence.

What Alexa doesn't know, but Sue does, is that I was born with artificial intelligence. For years I had been boring her (Sue, not Alexa) with my impressive knowledge of subject matter she considers trivial but which I maintain is invaluable to the well-being of society.

That includes my greatest area of expertise: the Three Stooges.

I proudly know, for example, that Curly's real name was — this is absolutely true — Jerry.

"That's not useless information, toots!" I once told Sue. "Nyuk, nyuk, nyuk!"

She has come to appreciate my knowledge of stuff nobody else cares about. And I have come to appreciate her knowledge of stuff she learned (but I seldom studied) in school.

Together, Sue and I are an unbeatable team in Question of the Day, mainly because we play alone and have no competition.

We began playing a few weeks ago for what I admit was a trivial reason: We had nothing better to do. Pretty soon, we were hooked.

Now, every day at lunch, unless we aren't home or we forget, in which case we are out to lunch, Sue and I are put to the test.

"Alexa," Sue will say, "what's the Question of the Day?"

"Welcome back to Question of the Day, your daily trivia challenge," Alexa will respond in her pleasant disembodied voice.

Then she will tell us in which of the game's six categories — arts and entertainment, science, literature, geography, general knowledge, and history — she will quiz us and how many points the question is worth. The higher the number (ten is tops), the harder the question.

If we answer correctly, we get a bonus question. Sometimes we get that one right, too, and rack up even more points.

If we answer incorrectly, I am usually to blame.

"I was going to say (a)," Sue will tell me after I have wrongly guessed (b).

"To (b) or not to (b)?" I asked one day.

"That's not the question," Sue answered.

Recently, our point total was nine hundred and ninety-eight.

"We're two points away from one thousand!" I said excitedly.

Sue summoned Alexa, who posed this question: "Which of the following is not considered to be one of the Seven Wonders of the Ancient World?"

The choices:

(a) Taj Mahal

(b) Lighthouse of Alexandria

(c) Colossus of Rhodes

(d) Great Pyramid of Giza.

If I guessed (b), I'd be Lightheaded, (c) I wouldn't be a Rhodes scholar, or (d) I'd be banished to the Great Pyramid of Geezer. So, in consultation with Sue, I went with (a).

"Good job!" Alexa exclaimed.

After giving us some interesting facts about the Taj Mahal (it was built in the mid-seventeenth century and is considered one of the Wonders of the Modern World) and informing us that only forty-seven percent of previous players got this question right, Alexa said, "You have reached a milestone — your one thousandth point in Question of the Day. Congratulations!"

We celebrated by treating each other to lunch at the kitchen table. Sue had an apple and I had a peanut butter sandwich.

"You can't say I'm an encyclopedia of useless information now," I said.

"I guess not," she conceded.

"And if you think that's impressive," I bragged, "just wait until Alexa asks me a question about the Three Stooges."

"Some People Have All the Luck"

I'm lucky I haven't won Mega Millions, Powerball, or even Lucky 7s. If I did, I'd keel over from shock and never cash in.

That is why I'm also lucky to have received a boxful of fun and intriguing items from Luck Shop, a business specializing in the kind of fabulous merchandise that promises riches, love, and other good things for people lucky enough not to drop dead upon learning they have hit the jackpot.

That merchandise, which can be found at luckshop.com, includes rabbit's feet, mojo bags, candles, lamps, oils, powders, perfumes, soap, incense, necklaces, and coins, all guaranteed to ward off evil and other nettlesome problems.

It was, of course, sheer luck that I stumbled upon an ad in the Old Farmer's Almanac for the Chicago-based company. Hoping to ward off evil, or at least car trouble, I called Luck Shop's owner, Ted Paspalas, a personable guy who is surrounded by stuff that could make him rich.

"Have you ever won Powerball?" I asked.

"If I did," Ted replied, "I wouldn't be sitting here talking with you. I'd buy a ticket to a Caribbean island. In fact, I don't even play the lottery."

"I do once in a while," I said. "But even if I won and lived to collect, all that money would only weigh down my pants and put me in a higher tax bracket."

Ted knows all about taxes because, in addition to being a successful entrepreneur, he's a certified public accountant.

"As a mathematician at heart, I know the odds are stacked against you," he said. "But if you believe that a coin or a rabbit's foot will bring you luck, more power to you. And sometimes it does work out."

That is evidenced by the many glowing testimonials Ted has received from satisfied customers.

Here are just three of them.

Tamika: "The Genie Lamp gave my enemies revenge for what they did to me and it also brought me good luck! I won $75 on Tuesday and $4,577 on Wednesday! THANK YOU!"

Laura: "My mom tried your Send Back Evil Powder two days ago. She applied the powder on the back of her neck and her stiff neck pain disappeared immediately!"

Cloretha: "I've been having the best days of my life thanks to you guys and these wonderful products. I wish I had known about you guys before my boyfriend got incarcerated."

"We get tons of unsolicited testimonials," said Ted, who is sixty-one and whose grandfather started the family business.

"I can see why," I said. "What's your favorite product?"

"The Genie Wishing Lamp," Ted replied.

"Does Barbara Eden pop out?" I wondered.

"No," said Ted. "I think she's retired."

"I noticed the Lucky Mojo Coin in the almanac ad," I said. "It might help me strike it rich in Powerball."

"If you win, I'm going to advertise you all over the world," Ted promised. "You'll be my best testimonial."

A week later, a small box arrived in the mail from Luck Shop. The box contained a Lucky Mojo Coin, a bottle of Extra

Strong Fast Luck Blessed Oil, a Blessed Gold Rabbit's Foot, a Rose Quartz Stone, a bottle of Spirit Blessed Oil, a Spiritual and Body Cleansing Bag, a package of Fast Money Bath Salt, and a bar of Reversible Turn Back Evil Soap.

"We're in the money now!" I told Sue. "Let's buy lottery tickets!"

I put the Lucky Mojo Coin in my pocket and drove with Sue to a nearby store, where I purchased a ticket for Mega Millions, which was being drawn that night, and a ticket for Powerball, which was being drawn the following night.

"And get a Lucky 7 scratch-off ticket," said Sue, who waited in the car.

When I came back out, Sue used a dime to scratch off her Lucky 7 ticket.

"Nothing," she sighed.

Not one number came up in Mega Millions, either. Nor in Powerball.

"So much for your good-luck charms," Sue said.

"On the contrary, I'm a lucky man," I declared. "At least I didn't drop dead."

"That's the Ticket"

I've got a ticket to hide. Actually, I've got four tickets that the Connecticut Department of Motor Vehicles thought I was trying to hide.

I plead ignorance, which I can say about practically any situation that involves me, because the parking citations were issued for a car that didn't belong to me, in a place where I no longer lived, at a time dating back to the turn of the century.

The mystery began when I received a letter from a

collection agency informing me that the vehicle in question received four parking citations, totaling a hundred and twenty dollars, in Bridgeport, Connecticut, in September 2002, October 2002, May 2003, and November 2003.

Curious as to why it took so long to get hold of me, and wondering if anyone who owned a Model T was also on the list, I called the collection agency and spoke with a nice person named Sarah.

I explained that I have never owned a car of that make and model and that it wasn't registered to me. I added that while I was born and raised in Stamford, Connecticut, I moved to Long Island, New York, in 1998.

"The account is still collectible," Sarah said.

"If it takes me twenty years to pay the tickets, would that be OK?" I asked.

"I can't give you any legal advice," Sarah told me, "but if this isn't you, contact the state DMV."

I called and, after being on hold for about the length of time it would take to drive to Connecticut, spoke with a friendly young woman named Taylor, who said, "When we have people who inquire about tickets that weren't for them, I direct them to the tickets department. Unfortunately, I don't have a number for them. They only communicate through email."

After Taylor gave me the email address, I asked, "Have you ever gotten a ticket?"

"No," she said proudly. "I don't have any parking violations or speeding tickets. I'm very careful."

Duly impressed, I thanked Taylor and sent the following email to the Connecticut Department of Motor Vehicles.

Dear DMV:

I recently received a letter from a collection agency about four parking tickets for a vehicle I never owned. Not only that, but the tickets, issued in Bridgeport and totaling a hundred and twenty dollars, were from 2002 and 2003. That's twenty years ago!

I suspect that the car belonged to my daughter and that I co-signed the loan. Frankly, my name must be on half the documents in the United States. I'm surprised the matter didn't come up during the debt negotiations.

Anyway, here are my questions:

Since the car technically wasn't mine, do I have to pay the tickets?

Isn't there a statute of limitations on this sort of thing?

If not, will you give me twenty years to clear it up?

Speaking of the time lag, why did it take the DMV so long to pursue the issue?

I am now sixty-nine. I will turn seventy in January. I think a nice seventieth birthday present from you to me would be to drop the whole stupid thing. I'll use the hundred and twenty dollars to buy myself something. Or I'll put it toward my car loan.

If you insist I pay the tickets, I will take the same amount of time you took to send this matter to a collection agency. That means I will be nearing ninety. I may not even be around then, in which case you should contact my daughter. Good luck getting money from her.

Thanks, DMV. I look forward to hearing back from you. Till then, take care, buy a calendar for the office, and watch where you park.

Sincerely,

Jerry Zezima

I received an email response from Ramon, who said the DMV doesn't have any record of the car being registered in my name and that my email was forwarded to the Bridgeport Parking Authority.

I called the authority and spoke with a pleasant and helpful person named Giselle, who said, "In Connecticut, parking tickets do not have a statute of limitations. The farthest back I could find was 1990. Unfortunately, the city of Bridgeport was a hundred million dollars in debt for parking tickets."

"I've put two daughters through college, including the one who owned the car that was ticketed, and I'm a hundred million dollars in debt," I said.

Giselle laughed and admitted that she once got a parking ticket.

"I could say I'm guilty," she said. "But I took responsibility and paid it."

Giselle added, much to my relief, that I'm not guilty.

"I'm emailing the collection agency," she said. "It will be taken care of."

"After all these years, I'm off the hook?" I said.

"Yes," Giselle replied. "But if you come back to Connecticut, be careful where you park. You don't want to get a ticket."

"A Second Helping of a Winning Recipe"

Even though I can barely make scrambled eggs, which become scrambled when I try to make fried eggs, I am more than just a flash in the pan.

That's why I am celebrating the twenty-fifth anniversary of my supreme culinary triumph, a dish called Zezima's Zesty Ziti

Zinger, which not only was first runner-up in the pasta sauce division of the 1998 Newman's Own & Good Housekeeping Recipe Contest, but earned raves from legendary actor Paul Newman, who wolfed down a bowl of the stuff after I assured him that it didn't kill my dog.

The previous year, someone from the Newman's Own office in Westport, Connecticut, called to ask if I would like to play the impossibly handsome movie star in a game of ping-pong at the Rainbow Room in New York City, where a luncheon for the recipe contest winners was being held.

I happily accepted, not so much because I would get a celebrity interview, but because I would get a free lunch.

In front of a crowd of about a hundred people, including notables such as Regis Philbin and Kathie Lee Gifford, I stood at one end of a ping-pong table and Paul Newman stood at the other. We each held a paddle.

A woman from the Newman's Own office, dressed in a black and white striped shirt, was the referee.

Newman hit my first serve into the net.

"Point, Mr. Newman," the ref said to gales of laughter from the audience.

He hit another shot long.

"Point, Mr. Newman."

I quickly realized that this guy's propensity for cheating was even greater than mine. But I admired him because his food company donated all of its after-tax profits to charity and the rigged game was for a good cause.

Later, Newman told me, "You should enter next year's recipe contest."

So I did. I concocted Zezima's Zesty Ziti Zinger following contest rules, which stated that at least one ingredient had to be a

Newman's Own product.

I used two jars of the company's spaghetti sauce. I also used chicken, hot sausage, garlic, a green pepper, an onion, crushed red pepper, salt, black pepper, basil, and half a cup each of red wine and vodka. It all went over a bed of ziti.

To my astonishment, my recipe finished second in a field of thousands, so I brought a bowl of the stuff to the following year's luncheon for Newman to try.

"Looks good, kid," he said, fork in hand.

"It is," I said. "I even gave some to my dog."

Newman paused and asked, "Is your dog still alive?"

"Yes," I answered.

His famous blue eyes twinkled. Then he scarfed it down and lived for me to tell about it.

Now, a quarter of a century later, I figured it was time to resurrect the recipe.

I made another batch of Zezima's Zesty Ziti Zinger and, with my wife's guidance, did not burn the house down.

"I like it," said Sue, who was, appropriately, the sous-chef. "It's a little spicy, but I really like it. You outdid yourself."

Unfortunately, Paul Newman wasn't around to try it again because he died in 2008. And not from a delayed reaction to food poisoning.

So I brought a container of Zezima's Zesty Ziti Zinger to Rocco's Ristorante, my favorite Italian eatery.

"It's good," said owner Paul DiGirolomo. "It's got a nice little kick to it."

"Is it good enough to put on the menu?" I asked.

"We have our own recipes," he answered. "But this one is a

winner."

Finally, I took a container to the ultimate arbiter: my mother.

"This is really good!" she exclaimed.

"You like it?" I said.

"If it was good enough for Paul Newman," my mother replied with a satisfied smile, "it's good enough for me."

CHAPTER 9:

"THE ICING ON THE CAKE"

"All Aboard the Polar Express"

On a December eve, very recently, I stood outside in the cold darkness dressed in my pajamas — and not for the first time, for I frequently go out in my PJs, much to the consternation of neighbors, shopkeepers, and, not least of all, the police.

Anyway, there I waited, amid a gathering crowd on a train platform, when I heard a conductor cry out, "All aboard!"

I ran up to him.

"Well," he said, "are you coming?"

"Where?" I asked.

"Why, to the North Pole, of course," was his answer. "This is the Polar Express."

And so it was. I was among countless excited ticket holders, young and old, who boarded the train in Kingston, New York, for a trip to the home of Santa and his elves. They would also be on board and, unbeknownst to them, would have to listen to my silly wisecracks as they mingled with the passengers. I'm lucky I didn't end up on the bad-boy list.

Accompanying me were Sue, Lauren, Guillaume, and, of course, Chloe and Lilly, who are most definitely on the good-girl list.

The train was filled with other children, their parents, and, on this special trip, their grandparents, all in their pajamas.

Chloe also wore a Santa hat and Lilly wore a conductor's cap.

When the real conductor, Jay, came by to punch our golden tickets, he noticed Lilly and allowed her to punch her own ticket because, of course, she was a conductor, too.

"I don't have a ticket," I confessed. "I snuck on the train."

Jay knew it was a fib, so he smiled and said, "I could throw you off, but I won't."

Then he punched my ticket and, with a hearty chuckle, added a smiley face.

Hero Boy, one of the characters in the famous book by Chris Van Allsburg, came by in a bathrobe with a hole in the pocket.

"I have a hole in my head," I told him. "And I go out in my pajamas all the time."

Hero Boy smiled weakly and said, "Merry Christmas!"

Then, wisely, he moved on down the aisle.

Next came a character from the film version of the book, the Hobo, who asked, "Do you believe in Santa Claus?"

"Of course!" I exclaimed. "In fact, I'm almost as old as he is. We hung out together as kids."

The Hobo chuckled and moved on, too.

A guy named Justin, dressed in a white chef's outfit, walked up with "The Polar Express" in his hands and asked me to turn the page as the story was being read over the loudspeaker.

"I write books, too," I told Justin. "Maybe my next one should be 'The Geezer Express.' "

An elf named Camilla stopped by with hot cocoa, which I slurped, and cookies, which I munched.

"Did you bake these cookies yourself?" I asked.

"Yes, I did," Camilla responded with a sly smile. "Honest!"

When she came back with bells for the passengers, I shook mine and said, "Camilla, your name rings a bell."

Just then, the jolly old elf himself, Santa Claus, made an appearance, which thrilled Chloe and Lilly, who told him what they wanted for Christmas. They also posed for a picture with him.

When Santa got to Sue and me, he asked, "And what do you want for Christmas?"

Sue said, "How would you like to pay off our mortgage?"

"Ho, ho, ho!" the big guy boomed.

"I'll take a bottle of brandy to celebrate getting out of debt," I told him.

Then I posed for a picture with Santa, too.

A little while later, the Polar Express pulled back into the station. It was a magical ride.

"Thanks for not throwing me off the train," I told the conductor on the way out.

"It's my Christmas present to you," he said. "And by the way, nice pajamas."

"Flaky the Snowman"

Once upon a time, in the frozen wastes of a suburban backyard that was buried under two feet of snow after a monumental blizzard, there lived Flaky the Snowman, who was so puny, so pathetic, but still so lovable that he could melt your heart if you met him.

I not only met this snowman, I made him with my own

hands. As Sue said after the flaky guy was finished, "Frosty would be embarrassed to be seen with him."

Since I was suffering from brain freeze, which happened quickly because my brain is the size of an ice cube, and inspired by the famous "Frosty the Snowman" tune, I came up with a song for the little fellow:

Flaky the Snowman

Was a silly lump of ice.

With a pair of shades and a floppy hat,

He was dumb and short and nice.

And little he was: one-foot-three in his stocking feet. Or he would have been if he had feet.

I envisioned a much larger creation when I trudged through my winter blunderland in the hope of building a snowman that would become a legend in my own mind.

The problem, I immediately found out, was that the snow was powdery. That's fine for skiing (I never took up the sport, even though I've been going downhill for years), but it wasn't so good for packing and rolling the three balls — large bottom, medium midsection, and small head — needed to make a perfectly proportioned precipitation person.

The fact that I hadn't built a snowman since woolly mammoths roamed the earth didn't help matters.

But I was determined to create a cool dude that would impress neighbors, visitors, or anyone who didn't mistake him for a burglar and call the cops.

I started by gathering the stuff I would need for limbs and facial features. For the limbs I chose — you guessed it — limbs.

Actually, they were a pair of twigs that Sue broke off a fallen tree branch. She also gave me a carrot for the nose and a bunch of purple fish bowl pebbles for the mouth. For the eyes, I got two wine corks on which I drew pupils.

The finishing touches were a pair of sunglasses and a hat like the one Bill Murray wore in "Caddyshack."

Now all I had to do was make the body.

"I can't pack the snow," I told Sue.

"You have to roll it into a ball," she said.

"It's falling apart," I complained.

Suddenly, a rare thought crossed my cranium and I snapped my fingers, which didn't work because I was wearing gloves.

I got a watering can, filled it with vodka (sorry, I mean water), and poured the liquid over a patch of snow.

I couldn't get the ball rolling, but I managed to pack enough snow for a lumpy base. Then I made a misshapen head and attached it to the deformed body.

The snowman couldn't give me the cold shoulder because he didn't have one.

But he did have arthritic arms (the twigs), an orange nose (the carrot), and a sly smile (another twig, which replaced the totally unusable pebbles).

I ditched the cork eyes and stuck on the shades. Then I topped him off with the hat.

"Your snowman has nothing on Frosty," Sue declared.

But he did impress a couple of young guys who came over to clear the driveway and shovel the walks.

"He's great," said Justin Felix, twenty, who co-owns North Coram Snow Removal. "Just like people, snowmen come in all shapes and sizes."

"He's pretty cool," said Matthew Owens, also twenty. "I like the hat and the nose. And the shades are a nice touch."

The next day, a cable company contractor arrived to take care of a sagging wire.

"That's a nice little snowman," said Ryan Howell, twenty-three. "It's better than what I could do. I've never made one. You did a good job."

A few days later, rising temperatures and falling rain spelled the end for Flaky.

I looked out the window and sang:

Flaky the Snowman

Was a puny guy, I'd say.

But we had some fun, he was number one.

He'd beat Frosty any day.

"How Sweet It Was"

It's a good thing I'm not a business magnate because I couldn't sell refrigerators in Death Valley. If I could, I'd be a refrigerator magnate.

But it turns out that I can sell peppermint pretzels and mint truffles. And I did, in astonishing amounts, when I worked for two days as a brand ambassador at Costco.

I got the idea to be one of those nice folks who give out food samples at the big-box retail stores when Sue said that if I went shopping with her, she would buy me lunch.

Sparing no expense, Sue shelled out $1.50 so I could have a hot dog and a soft drink in exchange for pushing a cart that was filled with cereal, toilet tissue, and so many other household items that I felt like a trucker who had flunked his driver's test.

On our rounds of the store, which is approximately the size of an airport terminal, except without the luggage carousels, I encountered a friendly guy named Gerald, who was giving out samples of white rice with soy sauce.

"Do you like your job?" I asked.

"I love it," replied Gerald, who is retired. "It gets me out of the house. And I'm doing something constructive."

"I'm retired, but I seldom do anything constructive, which is why my wife wouldn't mind it if I got out of the house," I said.

Sue nodded.

"I'm going to apply," I told her.

The process was long and complicated, requiring me to furnish so much information that I was shocked it didn't include my underwear size. I felt like I was applying for a job with the CIA, which in my case would stand for Comically Inept Associate.

But it was worth the trouble after I met Saima Iqbal, a very pleasant event manager for CDS (Club Demonstration Services), the company that hires the people who give out food samples at Costco.

After informing me that I had somehow made it through the application process and was being hired — at minimum wage, working six-hour shifts with a half-hour food break and another break of fifteen minutes — Saima gave me a blue apron, a CDS visor, and a name tag with JERRY in bold letters. Below that was my title: "Sales advisor."

"This will get me out of my wife's hair," I said.

Speaking of which, I had to wear a hair net and a face covering for my mustache. Also, I was required to wear disposable gloves. And I was shown how to prepare a food cart for selling products and how to wash and sanitize the cart and other equipment afterward.

"We place a premium on cleanliness," said Saima, who started as a sales advisor eleven years ago. "There's room for advancement," she added. "But we are going to start you slow."

"Thanks," I said. "I've always been a little slow."

That meant I wouldn't be using a microwave or an oven to prepare food.

"My wife doesn't trust me in the kitchen," I said.

"You should also know that members, as our customers are called, may ask you where certain items are in the store," Saima warned.

"I don't know where anything is at home," I confessed.

"Don't worry about it," she said. "Your job is to sell. Good luck and welcome aboard!"

I began on a Sunday, which was very busy. My shift started at ten-thirty a.m. and lasted until five p.m.

Saima wasn't working, but I was in good hands with Melissa, a personable senior shift supervisor who showed me how to set up my big metal cart, which contained a bowl, a stand, and other necessary items, including the product, Snack Factory pretzel crisps with white creme and peppermint.

I had to put two pretzel crisps in a small paper cup and put several cups of them on a tray under the stand.

"Remind people that they're on sale," said Melissa, pointing to an adjacent display with dozens of bags of peppermint pretzels.

I was in the most highly trafficked location in the store, right near the checkout area, so members who were lined up with their carts, waiting to be checked out, stood in front of my cart.

"Wow, peppermint pretzels!" was the typical reaction from members young and old.

"They're sweet and salty! And they're on sale!" I gushed,

pointing to the $4.99 price tag.

"How much do they usually go for?" one woman asked.

"A hundred bucks a bag," I answered. "But there's a special deal today."

She laughed and put two bags in her shopping cart.

"They're selling like hotcakes," an older man said.

"Maybe I should sell them, too," I replied.

He smiled and took a bag from the display.

The peppermint pretzels, which ordinarily sold for $6.99, were indeed a hot item.

"They could sell themselves, but they can't talk," I told a nice mom.

Her small son wolfed down four of them.

"Yum!" he declared.

The hardest part was keeping up with demand. I had to open bag after bag, pour the pretzel crisps into a bowl, and put them in the small cups, which I then had to place on the trays.

As soon as I did, they were snatched up.

At the end of my shift, I was tired and my feet were sore, but I felt good.

"It was fun," I told Gerald, who helped me clean up.

My second — and last — day was Tuesday.

Again, I was working from ten-thirty a.m. to five p.m. This time, though, I was selling Utah (that's the brand) milk chocolate mint truffles, which are "individually wrapped." They were on sale for $6.99, a saving of three dollars.

Saima, who was back to work, was dismayed when I told her before my shift that I would be quitting because of a scheduling conflict and not any dissatisfaction with the job.

"That's too bad," she said. "You did great on Sunday and everyone likes you."

"This must be the shortest career ever," I said. "Will I be eligible for a pension?"

"Sure," Saima answered with a smile. "And you'll get a 401(k)."

"How about a going-away party?" I asked.

"Why not?" she said.

When I went to my previous post in the front of the store, a sales advisor named Lee, who was selling chocolate-covered almonds, told me I was in the wrong spot.

"You're supposed to be in the back near the freezers," she informed me. "Look for the display with your product."

"Sorry," I said.

"I don't mean to bust your chops," Lee said sympathetically.

"Don't worry," I replied. "I'm not selling chops."

I set up my cart and launched into my sales pitch: "These truffles are a sweet treat that's good to eat and can't be beat. And they have a hint of mint. I like saying that because it rhymes."

In addition to scarfing down samples and buying bags of truffles, a lot of people asked for directions.

"Where can I find milk?" a woman inquired.

"In cows," I told her.

A guy asked, "Where's Celsius?"

"On a thermometer," I answered.

"I mean the energy drink," he explained.

"I have no idea," I said.

Fortunately, both of them laughed.

One woman looked at a bag of truffles and said, "They're individually wrapped?"

"Yes," I said. "They were wrapped by individuals."

She laughed, too.

And they all bought the product.

Toward the end of my shift, Saima stopped by because she was leaving for the day.

"Goodbye," she said. "And thank you."

"How did I do?" I asked.

"Excellent," she said. "If you want to come back, let me know."

The experience was excellent, too, thanks in large part to my fellow sales advisors, most of them retirees, including Alfonso, Andrew, Aquib, Christina, David, Frances, Gerald, John, Jon, Lee, Marianne, Nieves, and Sondra. They were all very nice and extremely helpful.

Even without the peppermint pretzels and mint truffles, two bags of which I bought for Sue, it couldn't have been sweeter.

"Ice Cream Guy Keeps on on Truckin' "

If you want to impress the children in your life — in my case, that would be five grandkids who all have a sweet tooth — break the exciting news that you have arranged for them to own, free of charge, the coolest vehicle ever:

The neighborhood ice cream truck.

That's what I did for Chloe and Lilly, who would eat ice cream for breakfast, lunch, and dinner if only their parents, who sadly don't know the health benefits of vanilla soft serve with rainbow sprinkles, would let them.

The ice cream truck in my neighborhood is driven by Mr. Mike, a terrific guy who's as sweet as the stuff he sells.

"Permission to come aboard," I said to Mr. Mike after he stopped his truck in front of my house.

"Hop up!" he chirped, mercifully turning off the monotonous jingle that plays over and over while he rolls down the street.

"Doesn't that song drive you crazy?" I asked.

"I don't even hear it," said Mr. Mike, who has tuned out the tune, "Turkey in the Straw," in the twenty-three years it has blared from his truck. "But at home, the TV bothers me."

Not much else bothers Mr. Mike, who was born in Turkey.

"But not in the straw," he noted.

Inside the truck, I beheld a treasure trove of treats.

"You have enough to feed an army," I told Mr. Mike, who served in the Turkish army before coming to the United States in the 1990s.

"And I sample it every day," he said. "I taste the chocolate, the vanilla, everything. I even taste the milk to make sure it's fresh."

"I guess you like ice cream," I said.

"I love it," said Mr. Mike, who is forty-nine and has a slim physique. "In fact, my whole family is crazy for ice cream. My wife, my daughter, my niece, my nephew, my sister, my niece's kids — they all eat it."

"My grandchildren love it, too," I said. "Two of them are sisters and we go out for ice cream all the time."

"When I retire, I'll give them the ice cream truck," he said. "They can take over the business."

"They'd probably eat the profits," I noted, "but I'll tell them what you said."

Until then, Mr. Mike will continue working hard, although he intends to take time off in September so he and his wife can celebrate their thirtieth anniversary.

"I'm going to take her on a trip," he said.

"In the ice cream truck?" I asked.

"No, on a cruise ship," Mr. Mike said.

"I hope there's ice cream on the boat," I said, adding that my wife has a cup of ice cream every night after dinner. "She puts it in the microwave."

"What's your favorite?" Mr. Mike inquired.

"I like toasted almond bars, but I can't find them anymore, so I go with vanilla," I said.

"Coming right up!" said Mr. Mike, who gave me a cone of soft serve that he dipped in toasted almond topping.

"What a combo!" I exclaimed as cream and crumbs lodged in my mustache.

After I inhaled it, Mr. Mike let me pour a cone of vanilla soft serve that he dipped in cherry topping.

"Here's a magic trick I do for the kids," he said, holding the cone upside down and swinging it back and forth like a pendulum.

"The ice cream isn't flying all over the place," I said in wonderment.

"The secret is fresh milk," Mr. Mike told me.

"I won't try that in the house or my wife would kill me," I said.

Speaking of which, Mr. Mike once made a special delivery to a cemetery.

"A customer told me that his father loved ice cream," he recalled. "The father said to the son, 'When I die, I want everyone to have ice cream.' So I delivered ice cream to the funeral."

Then there was the guy who washed Mr. Mike's truck in his driveway in exchange for free ice cream.

"My customers are the best," Mr. Mike said. "We always joke around. They say to me, 'You're crazy, but we love you.' "

The following weekend, when Chloe and Lilly came over, I told them what Mr. Mike said about giving them the truck.

"Wow!" Chloe gushed. "That would be great."

"You can drive," Lilly told me. "And don't eat all our ice cream."

EPILOGUE

When I was a kid, in a bygone era when the summer air was filled with the sounds of baseballs being batted through neighbors' windows and the smells of exhaust belching from family station wagons, my friends and I would eagerly await the daily arrival of the Good Humor man, whose truck made its way down our street with its bells jingling merrily.

Those were the days when ice cream trucks didn't play the same monotonous tune over and over until people from blocks around were driven to the brink of madness.

No, it was a simpler time, when kids actually went outside with the express purpose of having fun, which often entailed leaving flaming bags of dog poop on the front porch of the crotchety old buzzard who lived down the street.

When there was a lull in the action, we kept an eye out for the Good Humor man. (The other eye was kept out for girls who treated us as if we had an advanced case of leprosy.)

And when the truck stopped in front of our houses, we rushed up to the open window and searched our pockets for twenty-five cents or whatever it cost for a cone of rock-hard vanilla or chocolate (no soft serve back then) or maybe a delicious ice cream sandwich.

My favorite was the toasted almond bar. I always ordered one, sometimes two if I had half a buck.

And the Good Humor man lived up to his name, accepting our nonsense with a warm smile that made him seem as nice as our dads, though he was probably counting the weeks until we went back to school.

Yes, those were the days.

As I got older (I still haven't grown up), I kept a taste for ice cream.

When I played Little League baseball (I think I got two hits in my entire career), I'd get an ice cream bar from a stand at the park.

In high school, I'd hang out at an ice cream shop where all the cool kids looked down their finely enameled noses at dweebs like me. I'd reciprocate by looking down my booger-encrusted nose at them.

In college, I'd get a vanilla cone after dinner in the cafeteria, where the food was so bad that — this is absolutely true — one guy's dog refused to eat a sloppy joe. But the pooch did love ice cream.

After Sue and I got married, we'd have ice cream (and an occasional cocktail) while sitting in folding chairs outside our apartment.

Then Katie and Lauren came along. When they were little, I would drive them to the Glenbrook railroad station in our hometown of Stamford, Connecticut, where we would board the train for a short ride on the spur line to neighboring New Canaan. Our destination: the Häagen-Dazs shop, which served gourmet ice cream. It was almost as good as Good Humor.

On one visit, we met Robert Vaughn, an actor who gained fame for playing a spy named Napoleon Solo on the hit 1960s TV series "The Man From U.N.C.L.E." He was a very nice man who happened to love ice cream. The girls didn't know who the hell he was.

The years passed, Katie and Lauren went through high school and college, and eventually got married to Dave and Guillaume. Then they had children who are, perhaps not coincidentally, our grandchildren.

When Chloe was two, on a visit to Nini and Poppie's house, she met Christos Skartsiaris, who was then our neighborhood ice cream man.

"Hello, beautiful girl," Chris said as he scooped (of course) Chloe into his arms.

"Say hi," Lauren urged her.

"Hi," Chloe said tentatively.

Chris put her down and showed her his rolling office. Chloe was fascinated.

"She's like a kid in an ice cream truck," I said.

Chloe had the time of her life — and an ice cream pop.

"What do you say to Chris?" Lauren asked Chloe.

"Thank you," she said.

"You're welcome, sweetheart," said Chris, who was sweet, too.

It was Chloe's introduction to the treat she has always loved.

A couple of years later, I took her to Magic Fountain, a popular shop in Mattituck, New York, to make ice cream.

The owner, Choudry Ali, led us to the back.

"I'm going to need your help to make the next batch," he told Chloe, who was busy eating a cone of vanilla soft serve with rainbow sprinkles, which he gave to her as prepayment for her manufacturing services.

The next batch was honey-cinnamon. Chloe helped pour a bottle of honey into a plastic container. She also helped pour eight ounces of ground cinnamon into a measuring cup and dump the ingredients into the container.

Ali, who goes by his last name because "it's easier," squeezed in a bag of ice cream mix.

Chloe gave the bag a squeeze, too, then helped turn on the machine.

Twenty minutes later, the ice cream was done.

Ali handed a small plastic spoon to Chloe, who scooped out some honey-cinnamon, put it in her mouth, and exclaimed, "Wow!"

"Is it good?" Ali asked.

"Yes!" chirped Chloe.

Ali also gave her a cup of vanilla and pistachio "for being such a good ice cream maker."

Chloe gave Ali a high-five and said, "Thank you!"

"You're welcome," Ali replied. "Now you can say you taught your grandfather how to make ice cream."

Lilly soon developed a sweet tooth as well and has since teamed with her big sister in asking me to take them to Magic Fountain and other local shops for ice cream.

It's the same when Sue and I see Xavier, Zoe, and Quinn, all of whom love ice cream, either at home or at their favorite shop.

When I was working, a Mister Softee truck would sometimes stop by the office, bringing back childhood memories of the Good Humor man. I would order a cone of vanilla soft serve, eat it slowly, and head back to my desk, useless for the rest of the day.

And Sue has ice cream for dessert almost every night, filling a small bowl of whatever flavor is at hand and nuking it in the microwave for a few seconds.

I could never see the purpose of heating ice cream. I prefer to wolf it down in its frozen form, the result being that my brain, or what's left of it, temporarily suffers from freezer burn.

Needless to say, but I'll say it anyway, ice cream is a Zezima family tradition. I bet it's a tradition in your family, too.

Ice cream won't solve all the world's problems, but it does make tough times easier to take. So does a good sense of humor.

Erma Bombeck wrote, "If you can't make it better, you can laugh at it."

I hope this book has helped you do just that.

Yes, laughter is the best medicine. Love conquers all. And, as my grandkids would add, don't forget ice cream.